FANATICAL MILITARY RECRUITING

THE ULTIMATE GUIDE TO LEVERAGING
HIGH-IMPACT PROSPECTING TO ENGAGE
QUALIFIED APPLICANTS, WIN THE WAR FOR
TALENT, AND MAKE MISSION FAST

JEB BLOUNT

WILEY

Published by John Wiley & Sons, Inc., Hoboken, New Jersey.
Published simultaneously in Canada.

For general information on our other products and services or for technical support, please contact our Customer Care Department within the United States at (800) 762-2974, outside the United States at (317) 572-3993 or fax (317) 572-4002.

Wiley publishes in a variety of print and electronic formats and by print-on-demand. Some material included with standard print versions of this book may not be included in e-books or in print-on-demand. If this book refers to media such as a CD or DVD that is not included in the version you purchased, you may download this material at http://booksupport.wiley.com. For more information about Wiley products, visit www.wiley.com.

Library of Congress Cataloging-in-Publication Data:

Names: Blount, Jeb, author.
Title: Fanatical military recruiting : the ultimate guide to leveraging high-impact prospecting to engage qualified applicants win the war for talent, and make mission fast / Jeb Blount.
Description: Hoboken : Wiley, 2019. | Includes index.
Identifiers: LCCN 2018042080 (print) | LCCN 2018055283 (ebook) | ISBN 9781119473633 (Adobe PDF) | ISBN 9781119473626 (ePub) | ISBN 9781119473640 (hardback) | ISBN 9781119473633 (ePDF)
Subjects: LCSH: United States—Armed Forces—Recruiting, enlistment, etc. | BISAC: BUSINESS & ECONOMICS / Training. | BUSINESS & ECONOMICS / Development / General. | BUSINESS & ECONOMICS / Organizational Development.
Classification: LCC UB323 (ebook) | LCC UB323.B5962019 (print) | DDC 355.2/230973—dc23
LC record available at https://lccn.loc.gov/2018042080

Printed in the United States of America
V10007892_012919

For the men and women who work tirelessly to win the War for Talent for the United States Armed Forces. We are forever in your debt. Without you, there is no military, there is no freedom, there is no beacon on the hill, there is no American dream—everything we have, love, and hold dear. Our way of life, freedom to be, do, believe, and say anything we choose, is because of you.

Contents

Contents

I Go to Basic

Failure to adequately resource our [military] with the required number and quality of personnel can have far reaching and strategic implications and threaten our nation's ability to defend its national interests at home and abroad.

—Colonel Michael Matthews, United States Army

Shortly after my book *Fanatical Prospecting* was published, we began to get calls from military recruiting commands. They were ordering as many as 50 books at a time. At first we thought it was an anomaly, but the orders kept coming.

Then, I began getting e-mail and notes on social media from military recruiters and leaders telling me how they were using the techniques in *Fanatical Prospecting* to fill the recruiting funnel. Entire companies and battalions were reading the book. I couldn't make sense of why there was so much interest from the military in a prospecting book that was written primarily for business-to-business sales professionals.

A Conundrum

Sales Gravy, the company I founded in 2006, is a global training, development, and consulting company with a focus on business-to-business sales acceleration. We're known for helping our clients make sales productivity and performance improvements, fast. We've built our reputation on shaping and customizing training curriculum around our clients' unique situations and cultures.

We believe, at the core, that delivering training content in our clients' language is the most effective way to speed the pace of the assimilation and actualization of concepts and skills in the real world.

So, when the requests started pouring in from military recruiting leaders for Fanatical Prospecting training, we found ourselves in a conundrum—we knew nothing about the military recruiting process and had no foundational knowledge on how the military worked.

We know exactly what we're doing when civilian companies call us for help. We know the language of business. We speak sales and the sales process. It's in our DNA. We aren't starting from scratch.

The US military, though, was a complete unknown. Suddenly we were out of our comfort zone. We didn't know the language of the United States Armed Forces.

I grew up in Augusta, Georgia, near Fort Gordon. Many of my childhood friends were from military families. One of my best friends joined the Marines right out of high school. Another joined the Navy. My wife's dad was in the US Army Special Forces. She was an Army brat who was born on base. My dad was a Marine. He used the GI Bill to pay for college and became a lawyer.

Even with these connections, the military might as well have been a foreign country. I was ignorant, and this caused a level of stress and anxiety that I never experience with my civilian clients. Honestly, it is embarrassing to admit how little I knew about how the military worked—especially recruiting.

I was certain, though, that should we attempt to shove civilian sales techniques down the throats of military recruiters, we'd lose all credibility and make little impact. We'd be dismissed as just another group of civilians who "didn't get it."

Learning the Language

My "basic training" began at Fort Harrison in Helena, Montana, when Command Sergeant Major Rick Haerter took me under his wing. He spent hours getting me up to speed and changed my entire view of military recruiting.

Over the ensuing months I continued my education. I met dozens of officers and NCOs who were eager to help me learn. Captain Liz Alberton allowed me access to her entire company of recruiters and arranged a once-in-a-lifetime chance for me to jump with the Golden Knights. Command Sergeant Major Shawn Lewis guided my learning and gave me an opportunity to hone the FMR message with his battalion.

I have a stack of napkins filled with notes that I took while learning about military recruiting over beers with leaders like First Sergeant Michael Downing and First Sergeant Christopher Llewellyn, who graciously helped me understand the life of a military recruiter.

I also had the privilege of visiting the US Army Recruiting and Retention College at Fort Knox with Sergeant First Class James Beaty, where I was able to meet the instructors and observe and participate in classes. Sergeant First Class Beaty invested hours, patiently teaching me how recruiting works and how to speak military language.

It was following a Fanatical Military Recruiting Boot Camp in Nashville, Tennessee, when the battalion commander exclaimed, "If I didn't know the truth, I'd have believed that you'd been a career recruiter" that I knew I'd passed the first test. With the help of many kind people, I was learning the language and battle rhythm of military recruiting.

Military Recruiting versus Civilian Sales

Through my "basic training" I developed a new appreciation for the role the military recruiter plays in building and maintaining strength of force. I gained deep respect for the price they and their families pay for mission. I was also confronted with the unique challenges recruiters and their leaders face. I learned:

1. Military recruiting is among the most difficult tours. The stress and pressure to perform is unrelenting.
2. Most military recruiters and their leaders adhere to an NCO Creed, take their mission seriously, and are eager to learn, grow, develop, and become better at their craft.
3. The various branches of the military invest heavily in training new recruiters. This foundational training helps green recruiters gain basic competencies for recruiting.
4. Despite the upfront training investment, most military recruiters begin their new role unprepared for the demands of the job and are far outside of their comfort zone.
5. Almost nothing in the military prepares recruiters for the emotional rigors, interpersonal skills, time management, and prospecting discipline required for high performance. No one "joins" the military to be a recruiter.
6. Military recruiters and their leaders recognize that they need more than basic recruiting training to perform at a high level. They see the need to consistently build on and improve recruiting skills. For this reason, they gravitate toward civilian sales books like my book *Fanatical Prospecting*.
7. Commercial sales and military recruiting are not the same. Although there are parallel skill sets between military recruiting and civilian sales, recruiting is a specialized endeavor that requires a specific set of competencies. Therefore, civilian sales processes don't necessarily translate and thus are difficult for military recruiters to assimilate.
8. Yet, outside of formal military recruiting school, there are few advanced, high-quality training resources designed *specifically* for the unique needs of military recruiters.

9. More is being demanded of recruiters than ever before. At the same time, the available pool of qualified prospects has decreased significantly,[1] and the competition in the marketplace for top talent, from all sectors, has accelerated.

10. Therefore, to win the War for Talent, today's military recruiters must operate at a level of excellence beyond anything asked of them in the past.

The more I interacted with military recruiters, the more my mind-set about their role in our democracy shifted. With the entirety of America's military strength resting on the strong shoulders of military recruiters, I found it abhorrent that the advanced training resources required for recruiters to grow, develop, and excel either didn't exist or were not readily available.

So, *my* mission changed. I became obsessed with developing *advanced military recruiting–specific* training that honors the special and important role played by military recruiters in keeping our armed forces strong and our country safe.

This book, *Fanatical Military Recruiting*, is the result of that mission shift. It is the first book in a three-book series that will include *Military Recruiting EQ* and *Coaching Military Recruiting*.

- *Fanatical Military Recruiting* focuses on top of the funnel activity—primarily prospecting.
- *Military Recruiting EQ* focuses on emotional intelligence, interpersonal skills, and the human influence frameworks required to engage highly qualified applicants and successfully move them through the recruiting process.
- *Coaching Military Recruiting* is a field guide for NCOICs that arms field level leaders with the unique tools, techniques, skills, and competencies for leading, developing, and coaching high-performance military recruiting teams.

I believe the timing is right for these new resources because military recruiting is facing a perfect storm. In this new paradigm, recruiters must quickly up-skill and gain new competencies to win the War for Talent.

Author's Note on Language: Throughout this book, I do my best to incorporate the terms, jargon, and language of military recruiting. The challenge I've faced is that each branch of the military has a unique and different language. For this reason, I've chosen to use generic terms that readers will understand and can easily translate to their own branch. In other cases, I've used my own language and descriptions because I'm unable to find a generic equivalent that connects with all readers and branches. It's an impossible task to be everything to everyone, so I humbly ask for your forgiveness where my terms may be confusing or I've gotten it wrong.

PART

I

Mission Critical

1 | Military Recruiting Is Facing a Perfect Storm

America without her soldiers would be like God without His angels.
—Claudia Pemberton

The military is no longer, and will never again be, the place of last resort for troubled and low-IQ members of our society. Military service has become an upwardly mobile career choice for the most gifted, talented, and intelligent among us.

Members of the military receive consistent pay raises, enlistment and retention bonuses, recession-proof job security, college tuition, guaranteed retirement income, and incredible benefits including paid housing, free health care, training, and paid education. They also have access to facilities on military bases that are unavailable to most civilians.

From a purely economic standpoint, joining the military is a smart financial move that gives a fortunate few access to a lifestyle and standard of living far above that of most civilians.

Yet deteriorating attention spans have made it difficult to get prospects to sit still long enough to learn about this incredible career opportunity. Meanwhile, fewer young Americans are interested in or even aware of the benefits afforded by a military career.[1]

Studies suggest that the majority of those who enlist and serve come from a family in which a parent or sibling is also in the military.[2] Yet the size of the active-duty US military is at its lowest level in more than 50 years.[3] With this, fewer young people than ever before have family members who are in the military or are learning about military life from influential mentors.

Worse, a high percentage of active-duty military members come from just five states—mostly the Southeast—with the Southern states consistently contributing the highest number of new recruits as a proportion of the population.[4]

Despite the incredible career opportunities available in the modern armed forces, military recruiters are increasingly operating in an America where there is a divide between the civilian and military classes.[5]

The pool of prospects with family or geographic associations to military service is steadily evaporating.[6] With increasing base closures and consolidations, fewer cities have a large military presence. This means young people are less likely to be exposed to military personnel beyond those they see online and in the media.

The connection between civilians and the military is eroding,[7] making it much more difficult for recruiters to engage prospects and their parents. "We speak a different language. We are governed by a separate set of norms and dogma. We even live apart from each other," says Phillip Carter of the nonpartisan think tank the Military, Veterans and Society Program at the Center for a New

American Security. He describes America's sprawling military bases as our "most exclusive gated communities."

This gap has extended to public schools and universities. Increasingly, faculty are ostracizing the military and its recruiters, either overtly or in more nuanced ways. These institutions, despite legal obligations to provide access, make it difficult for military recruiters to engage students, using either passive roadblocks or outright hostility to create de facto no-go zones.

Though the military is among the most trusted and revered American institutions,[8] in the words of Lieutenant Colonel Remi M. Hajjar, a professor at West Point, "Many Americans consider the military a bit like a guard dog. They are very thankful for the protection, but they probably wouldn't want to have it as a neighbor. And they certainly are not going to influence or inspire their own kids to join that pack of Rottweilers to protect America."

Qualification Standards Continue to Tighten

Meanwhile, as the available talent pool shrinks in the midst of this perfect storm, the military apparatus continues to tighten qualification standards, and politicians play games that strain recruiting budgets.

Still, even when recruiters identify qualified prospects who have a propensity for joining the military, they face another, daunting gauntlet. The prospects in this new generation have more power— more information, more distractions, more options, more at stake, and more control over their future—than at any time in history.

With so many options available for talented people, they can afford to wait for "something better to come along." This, combined with extreme information overload, creates fear and insecurity that often leaves prospects and their parents clinging to the status quo. Doing nothing, making no choice at all, is often their preferred course of action.

It's no wonder so many recruiters are struggling. It's no wonder that recruiting leaders are frustrated and more stressed out than ever. And it's not surprising that most recruiting units are staring down the barrel at 50 percent or more of their recruiters consistently missing mission.

This perfect storm of obstacles creates an existential threat to the strength and readiness of the greatest fighting force ever assembled on earth and may weaken its ability to protect our democracy.

If we've lost the benefit of historical family ties to military service, if our education system is a hindrance, if the gap between civilian society and the military is growing, and if young people have more options, feel less inclined to serve, and are ill informed on the benefits of military service—then our only hope lies with our military recruiters and their ability to close the gap.

This is why it is imperative that we arm our recruiters and NCOICs with the skills they need to win the war for talent in this challenging environment.

2

Nothing Prepared You for This War

The object of war is not to die for your country but to make the other bastard die for his.

—General George S. Patton

Recruiting is a war. Just a different kind of war than the one you prepared for and trained to fight. Recruiting is a War for Talent— for the hearts and minds of the next generation of talent that will protect and defend our country and way of life.

Rather than bullets and bombs, this War for Talent is won through disciplined use of time, intellectual agility, emotional intelligence, mastering your own disruptive emotions, leveraging human influence frameworks, and massive prospecting activity.

But make no mistake: The War for Talent is real. All organizations in America—businesses, health care, nonprofit groups, sports, education, and the military—are in an outright and never-ending battle to recruit and retain the brightest and most talented people.

Smart, competent, and capable people are rare and in high demand. You are competing with every other organization and your fellow recruiters from other armed services branches to gain the attention of and engage this talent. It's winner takes all. There is no good enough. There is no prize for second place. Once you lose prospects to your competition, the probability that you will ever get them back plunges.

On this highly competitive, ever-changing, asymmetric battlefield you must be at your best—always. If you:

- Allow your discipline to slip, you lose.
- Let your guard down, you lose.
- Whine about how hard things are, you lose.
- Get distracted, you lose.
- Get tired, put down your ruck, take a knee and rest awhile, you lose.
- Are unable to manage your emotions, you lose.
- Are undisciplined with time, you lose.
- Fail to execute a systematic and methodical daily battle rhythm, you lose.
- Fail to maintain focus and attention control, you lose.
- Are afraid to interrupt people and ask for what you want, you lose.
- Don't talk to enough people, you lose.

On Most Days, Recruiting Doesn't Feel Much Like Winning

You are a winner. You are the type of person who hits every target you put in front of your sights. That's how you landed this recruiting tour in the first place—you are among the most talented people in your branch of the military. The top tier. You are used to winning.

Yet on most days, military recruiting doesn't feel much like winning. You strike out a lot. You are rejected, told no, and pushed aside.

When you are used to winning, what seems like almost constant failure can be demoralizing. You feel out of your element and out of control. If you failed this much on any other tour, you'd be removed from the service.

But military recruiting is different. The competencies, mind-sets, and skills required for high performance in recruiting are different from almost anything else you've been asked to do in the military. Nothing you've done in your military career prepared you for this battle. For a Soldier, Sailor, Marine, Airman, or Guardsman, it is and will be the most demanding and unrelenting fight you will face.

Asymmetric Battlefield

In the War for Talent, the battlefield is nonconforming, ever shifting, and always changing. It is impossible to control and unpredictable. Every prospect, every applicant is different. Every day is different. You must adjust on the fly. You must be flexible. You must be agile.

Civilians

For the bulk of your career, you've interacted primarily with other people in the military. These people understand you and your language. There are rules of conduct, tradition, and respect. It's challenging but comfortable, because you know what to expect. In the military, there is predictability and stability. In recruiting, not so much.

Civilians—and their erratic and irrational decision making—control your destiny. Parents, educators, and especially teenagers don't understand you and at times don't respect you. Military recruiters have one foot in the military and one foot in the civilian world. It's no wonder why you feel like a schizophrenic at times.

Rejection

Before you deployed, the military trained and drilled you on how to function effectively on the battlefield and manage your emotions and behaviors while under fire. You received a weapons kit—a rifle, artillery, tanks, drones, aircraft, boats, grenades, and so forth. You rehearsed constantly to perfect a response to any situation you might encounter.

Whenever the enemy engaged you or you engaged the enemy, you knew exactly what to do. It may have been a chaotic two-way range, but your training kept you in control and in the fight, so you could shoot back.

In this role, you face a different type of bullet. *Rejection.* Nothing prepared you for the neuro-physical and psychological pain of rejection. No one taught you how to handle being rejected by a teenager, parent, educator, or administrator.

You can't shoot back, which makes it feel like you have little control. You cannot order people. Instead you must leverage interpersonal skills and/or influence frameworks to get them to comply with your requests.

Emotions

Recruiting requires emotional control and resilience. You learned to control your emotions in the heat of battle through constant training and repetition. With so much repetition, you didn't need to think, only act.

But nothing prepared you for the massive emotional roller coaster that is military recruiting. On this battlefield you must be aware of and control your own disruptive emotions while at the same time effectively perceiving and appropriately responding to the emotions of other people.

Independence and Mission Ownership

In virtually every role as you were coming up through the ranks from Private to NCO, you've worked in tight units and teams.

Every individual on that team depended on the other members. You worked as one unit, with one purpose—together.

In military recruiting, though, you spend most of your time away from your team members. You are on your own as you prospect, work your schools, interact in the community, and engage with parents in their homes. Depending on your branch and command, you may be penalized or rewarded for individual achievement.

Your leaders may tell you what to do and teach you how to do it. They can put policies in place, give out incentives, and force you to work, but it's impossible to order you to "recruit." Since you have so much independence, no one is standing over you, telling you what to do.

Instead, you've got to get your ass up and go out there and make things happen yourself. You've got to manage your own time, pick up the phone, meet parents, canvass for prospects, make presentations in classrooms, turn teachers into advocates, build relationships with community partners, ask for commitments, absorb insults, and accept endless rejection—on your own.

Only you can choose to adopt a fanatical military recruiting mind-set. Only you can choose to be relentless and unstoppable in your pursuit of mission. Only you can decide to win. You must make the personal choice to be excellent at your job and win the War for Talent.

Go look in the mirror. You own mission.

FMR versus What You Learned at the Schoolhouse

Remember when you went to boot camp? You were transformed from a civilian to a member of the military. You gained a foundational knowledge of your branch, expectations, military life, and working as a unit. But you were not ready or prepared to execute on the battlefield or for your MOS.

It was akin to being in first grade, where you learned the alphabet and how to add one plus two. You began building your vocabulary, but you weren't ready to write a college essay. It wasn't until you graduated from advanced training and then learned on the job that you began to master your role and responsibilities.

Likewise, when you became a recruiter, you were sent to recruiting school. At school, you gained the foundational knowledge required to earn your recruiting badge. You learned systems, processes, policies, and expectations. You learned the language of recruiting. You were given a manual. But the schoolhouse is not reality. It is the basics, the ABCs, first grade.

The truth is, it was difficult to learn at the schoolhouse because it was an overwhelming firehose of information shoved down your throat and many times you weren't actually listening. Most of what you've learned so far has been on the job.

Fanatical Military Recruiting begins where the recruiting and retention colleges and schools of the various branches of the military leave off. It's designed to hone and amplify what you've been learning OTJ.

Will many of the things we discuss sound similar to what you learned in basic recruiting school? Of course. The basics and fundamentals are always in play.

Fanatical Military Recruiting, though, is a masters in military recruiting. FMR is real life in the real world. There's no BS and no theory. You'll face the uncomfortable truth about why you are missing mission and exactly what it takes to make mission every month, without fail.

It all begins with a fanatical, relentless focus on prospecting.

3

Fanatical Prospecting

Let's keep it 100. If you had a choice between calling prospects and taking live fire, you would choose the bullets.

—Jeb Blount

Ultra-high-performing recruiters are relentless, unstoppable prospectors. They are obsessive about outmaneuvering their competition and keeping the funnel full of qualified prospects. They prospect anywhere and anytime—constantly kicking down doors looking for their next opportunity. They prospect day and night—they ask, and ask, and ask, until they get a qualified prospect to say *yes*.

Ultra-high performers (UHPs) are unstoppable and always on—fanatical. My favorite definition of the word fanatical is "motivated or characterized by an extreme, uncritical enthusiasm."

Top military recruiters view prospecting as a way of life. They prospect with single-minded focus, worrying little about what other people think of them. They enthusiastically dive into telephone prospecting, area canvassing, cold calling, networking, asking for referrals, social media, following up on leads, working schools, setting up at school and community events, and striking up conversations with strangers.

- They don't make excuses: "This is not a good time to call." "The system is down."
- They don't complain: "Nobody is calling me back." "The leads are bad."
- They don't whine: "Nobody answers the phone." "No one is qualified." "The other branches are offering a better deal."
- They don't live in fear: "What if she says no?" "What if this is a bad time?" "What if his dad answers the phone?"
- They don't procrastinate: "I don't have time right now. I'll catch up tomorrow."
- They prospect even when mission is made because they know that there is no time to rest.
- They prospect when times are bad because they know that prospecting is the key to survival.
- They prospect even when they don't feel like prospecting because they are driven to keep their recruiting pipeline full.

Fanatical military recruiters carry around a pocket full of business cards. They talk up strangers on the sidewalk, in grocery stores, at schools, at sporting events, in line to get coffee, in elevators, trains, buses, and anywhere else they can get face-to-face with potential recruits.

They get up in the morning and bang the phone. During the day they are networking at schools. In the evening they knock on doors. In between interviews they prospect with e-mail and text. At night they work social media. While applicants are being processed at MEPS, they grab a list, pick up the phone, and make more calls.

Before they quit for the day, they make even more attempts. The enduring mantra of the fanatical military recruiter is: *One more call.*

Prospecting is the air they breathe. They don't whine like babies about not having enough leads or cry about how MEPS is kicking back all of their applicants. Their survival does not rest on the hope for a CAT-4 day. They don't blame the command, MEPS, the prospects, parents, teachers, schools, news, or society. They get moving, take responsibility, and *own* mission. They generate their own leads and, through hard work, determination, and perseverance, their own luck.

Fanatical military recruiters are aware that failure in recruiting is not caused by a deficit of talent, skills, or training. Not a poor territory or inferior prospects. Not the other branches of the military. Not "this generation" of teenagers. Not the latest news cycle or the person currently occupying the White House. Not the NCOIC, First Sergeant, Sergeant Major, or anyone else in the chain of command.

The brutal fact is the number-one reason for failure in recruiting is an empty funnel, and the root cause of an empty funnel is the failure to prospect. The foundation of all success in recruiting is a fanatical focus on prospecting.

It's simple, the more people you talk to, the more people you'll enlist. The Pipe (funnel) is Life.

4

Stop Wishing Things Were Easier

The only easy day was yesterday.

—US Navy SEALs

There is no sugarcoating it. Prospecting means facing certain rejection. This is why so many recruiters don't do it and instead spend their time and energy seeking silver bullets, secret formulas, and shortcuts; or hanging out on social media; or ignoring prospecting altogether until they dig themselves deep into a hole; or wasting time with applicants who are disqualified.

The truth is prospecting is the hardest, most mentally exhausting part of your recruiting day. There will always be something more fun you would rather do, and it will never get easier. But the one thing that separates ultra-high performers from other recruiters is they look rejection in the face and do it anyway.

Here's the deal. If you want sustained success in your recruiting tour, if you want to consistently make mission, then you've got to

16

interrupt strangers—lots of them. The real reason that prospecting is so hard, no matter how you choose to do it, is that you are interrupting strangers. This, by the way, is why so many recruiters protest so loudly and will do almost anything to avoid making an outbound call.

It is difficult and awkward to interrupt someone's day. You can't control their response and that unknown leaves you feeling vulnerable and causes fear.

Your prospect's initial reaction to being interrupted—usually a brush-off or reflex response in a not-so-friendly tone of voice—feels like rejection. Sometimes it *is* rejection. They attack you, disrespect you, call you a baby killer, and put you down just for doing your job. This is the core reason mediocre recruiters spend most of their time finding excuses not to prospect rather than just doing it.

What they fail to understand is that interrupting and talking to people is the fundamental building block of robust recruiting funnels. If you don't interrupt strangers relentlessly, your funnel will be anemic, and you will fail.

There Is No Easy Button in Military Recruiting

"Lose weight effortlessly," the announcer says over an image of models admiring their ripped abs. "With this revolutionary breakthrough pill you'll never have to worry about your weight again. Eat what you want. Forget about exercise. Just take this pill and you'll have the body of your dreams."

If these commercials didn't work, the companies that run them would quit. But they *do* work. In his book *Spartan Up: A Take-No-Prisoners Guide to Overcoming Obstacles and Achieving Peak Performance*, Joe De Sena explains that "*easy* is the greatest marketing hook of all time."

So companies promise, again and again, that you can lose weight, flip houses, or get rich with no pain, no sacrifice, and no effort. Their phones ring off the hook, even though most people know intuitively that these promises are overhyped and not true. It's just human nature to seek the easy way out.

It is disappointing to observe how many recruiters have this same attitude—always looking for easy. They whine and complain endlessly about the job, leads, prospects, parents, MEPS, educators, their territory, the bureaucracy, their leaders, taking time away from their family, and on and on. They have somehow deluded themselves into believing that they are entitled to easy.

Here is a brutal truth: Military recruiting is not easy. It won't become easy. It will never be easy. Whether you volunteered or were voluntold, you have mission and a job to do, and it is and will be the hardest, most challenging period of your military career.

Military recruiting is not a nine-to-five job. There are no days off. No vacations. No lunch breaks. No rest. It's a single-day deployment *times* 365 for however long your tour lasts.

Ultra-high-performing military recruiters are always on, always recruiting, unstoppable—whatever it takes to make mission. Recruiting is tough, grueling, and sometimes heartbreaking work. The pressure is unrelenting.

Unlike other tours, in recruiting you have one number, and there is no place to hide. You must deliver results or suffer the consequences. In military recruiting, it's not about who you have enlisted—it is about who you enlist *today*. The threat of facing discipline because you have a bad month, quarter, or year is always hanging over your head.

Along with this unrelenting stress, military recruiters face endless rejection. You receive more rejection in a day than the average service member gets in an entire year. The fact is, most people wouldn't last a minute in your shoes. They are so afraid of rejection that they'd rather charge a bunker than make a single prospecting call.

Yet most people don't understand you or your role. They don't understand the stress. They don't understand that to achieve your goals you're working seven days a week, and on many of these days twelve to sixteen hours. On this duty you never take a knee.

In recruiting there will always be something to complain about. That's just how it is. Nothing is perfect. There will be obstacles, challenges, rude administrators, indecisive and unqualified prospects, out-of-touch parents, demanding leaders, constant changes to mission and what constitutes an acceptable applicant, and of course MEPS.

There will always be rejection. There will be people who protest against you, hate you even though you protect them, offend you with their words and actions, and never understand your purpose. There will always be changes to mission—usually asking you to give more.

Adopting a fanatical military recruiting mind-set is the difference between making your recruiting tour a rewarding, successful experience or just doing time and waiting for the bitter end. You can sit around and complain and whine, but trust me, you are only hurting yourself, your unit, your family, and ultimately, your country.

Get Better

Developing a fanatical military recruiting mind-set begins with coming to grips with and accepting that military recruiting is hard, grueling, rejection-dense work. There is no sugarcoating it. You have a tough job to do and most of the time it sucks.

So instead of whining about the things that are outside of your control, focus your energy on the only three things you can control:

1. Your actions
2. Your reactions
3. Your mind-set

The first step toward building an endless pipeline of new prospects and crushing mission is acknowledging the truth and stepping back from your emotional need to find Easy Street. In military recruiting, easy is the mother of mediocrity, and in your life, mediocrity is like a broke uncle. Once he moves into your house, it's nearly impossible to get him to leave.

Author and speaker Jim Rohn once said that you shouldn't wish that things were easier; you should, instead, wish that you were better. That's the promise I make to you. When you adopt the techniques in this book, *you will get better.*

You will become a more efficient recruiter. You will learn how to deliver mission in less time, so that you have more time for your family, friends, and enjoying life.

You will become a more effective recruiter. Prospects enlist with *you*—then the military. You will learn how to engage prospects in conversations, move them into your funnel as qualified applicants, get them to the floor, and generate more enlistments who ship. You'll gain powerful skills and techniques, deliver better results, and ultimately become the ultra-high-performing recruiter your leaders trust, praise, and award.

I will not lie or pander to you, though. I am not going to promise to make recruiting easier, take away the sting of rejection, or turn prospecting into something that you will learn to love. The techniques I teach you will not eliminate rejection, make recruiting painless, or remove the emotional pain of dealing with disrespectful teenagers, their helicopter parents, or rude educators.

Only you can make the decision to do the hard work, pick up the phone, approach strangers, and get past your own mental hang-ups. The choice to act, the choice to adopt a new Fanatical Military Recruiting mind-set, is yours and yours alone.

It's time to stop wishing it was easier and start working to make yourself better.

PART II

The Ask

5

Effective Recruiting Begins with the Discipline to Ask

The more people you talk to, the more enlistments you'll make.
—First Sergeant Christopher Llewellyn
(and First Sergeants everywhere)

Asking is the most important discipline in recruiting. Period. You must ask for what you want, directly, assumptively, assertively, and repeatedly. Asking is the key that unlocks:

- Qualifying information
- Meetings and interviews
- Access to students in schools
- Parental permission
- Next steps that move applicants through the funnel
- Getting applicants to the floor
- Enlistment commitments

In military recruiting, asking is everything. When you fail to ask, mission suffers. Your reputation suffers. Your unit suffers. You suffer. Your family suffers.

When you fail to ask, you fail. It's the truth, and this truth will not change. But, as my favorite line from the movie *The Big Short* goes, "The truth is like poetry. And most people fucking hate poetry."[1]

This is why immutable truths like "The more people you talk to, the more enlistments you'll make" are so easily ignored.

If you are having a hard time getting interviews, next steps, access to schools or homes, applicants to MEPS, and enlistments, it's not because you lack prospecting skills, closing skills, the right words to say, or tactics for getting past the inevitable objections.

Nope, you are not getting what you want because you are not *asking* for what you want. Why? Nine times out of 10, you are insecurely and passively beating around the bush because you are afraid to hear the word *no*.

In this state, confident and assumptive asking gets replaced with wishing, hoping, and wanting. You hesitate, use weak, passive words. Your tone of voice and body language exude insecurity and desperation. You wait for prospects to do your job for you and set the appointment, set the next step, or enlist themselves.

But they don't.

Instead, they resist and push back with objections. They put you off, brush you off, turn you off, and sometimes disrespect you. Your passive, insecure, fearful behavior only serves to encourage more resistance and rejection.

In military recruiting, passive doesn't work. Insecurity won't play. Wishing and hoping is not a viable strategy. Only confident, assumptive asking generates the outcomes you want.

Conjuring the Deepest, Darkest Human Fear

But asking with assumptive confidence is one of the most difficult things for humans to do. The assumptive ask requires you to put it all out there. An emotional risk, with no guarantees. When you ask with confidence, you make yourself instantly vulnerable, with no place to take cover.

Vulnerability, according to Dr. Brenè Brown, author of *The Power of Vulnerability*, is created in the presence of uncertainty, risk, and emotional exposure. This vulnerability conjures up the deepest and darkest of human fears:

The fear of rejection.

Rejection is a painful demotivator and the genesis of deep-rooted fear. Leading up to your *ask*, everything in your body and mind are screaming at you to *stop* as the anticipation of being rejected generates this deep sense of vulnerability.

The fear and avoidance of the emotional pain caused by rejection is why so many recruiters seek the easy way out. It's the top reason why recruiters fail to make mission. The fear of rejection is the most treacherous disruptive emotion for recruiters and the primary reason they aren't consistently prospecting.

Here are two brutal, undeniable truths (and we already know how people feel about the truth):

1. The *only* way to eliminate rejection is to *never ask for anything again. Ever.*
2. To be *successful* in military recruiting, you must ditch your wishbone and grow a backbone.

Everything depends on the discipline to *ask*.

6

How to Ask

Asking is the beginning of receiving.
　　　　　　　—Jim Rohn, author and motivational speaker

Starting with prospecting, while advancing your applicants through the recruiting process, and all the way through to enlistment, you must constantly be asking your prospects and applicants for commitments. To reduce resistance and get them to comply with your requests, you must ask confidently, concisely, and assertively, with no hesitation (see Figure 6.1). There are three keys to asking:

1. Ask with confidence and assume you will get what you want.
2. Shut up!
3. Be prepared to deal with objections.

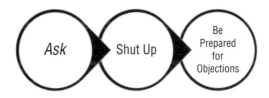

Figure 6.1 The three keys to asking.

Emotional Contagion: People Respond in Kind

Be intentional. Be decisive. Get to the point. When you are confident with your ask and assume you will get what you want, the probability increases exponentially that your prospect will respond in kind and comply with your request.

When recruiters ask with assertive confidence, qualified prospects say yes 50 to 70 percent of the time. Conversely, nonassertive, insecure, "I-don't-want-to-seem-too-pushy" requests have a 10 to 30 percent success rate.

In a weird paradox, when you try not to be "pushy" because you think it will turn prospects off, you trigger objections. When you sound and look afraid, when you give off an insecure vibe, you transfer that fear to your prospect and create resistance where it didn't previously exist.

One truth about human behavior is that people tend to respond in kind. "People are extremely good at picking up on other people's emotions—both negative and positive—without consciously trying," writes Shirley Wang in her article "Contagious Behavior." [1]

Emotional contagion is an automatic, subconscious response that causes humans to mirror or mimic the behaviors and emotions of those around them. It makes it very easy for humans to both feel what other humans are feeling and transfer emotions to other people. Knowing how to leverage emotional contagion is a powerful meta-skill for influencing human behavior.

When you are relaxed, confident, and assumptive, you transfer these emotions to your prospects, thus reducing resistance and objections. In turn, you get more wins, and with more wins your confidence grows.

The Assumptive Ask

Relaxed, assumptive confidence is the most powerful position for the military recruiter. Assuming that when you ask, you will get what you want creates a mind-set of positive expectation. This mind-set manifests itself in your outward body language, voice inflection, tone, and word patterns.

The foundation of the assumptive ask is your belief system and self-talk. When you tell yourself that you are going to win and keep telling yourself so, it bolsters your confidence and expectation for success. Ultra-high performers exude confidence. This confidence transfers to prospects, compelling them to comply with your requests.

I've spent most of my life around horses. Horses have an innate ability to sense fear. They test new riders and take advantage of them the moment they sense that a rider is afraid or lacks confidence. Horses have a 10-to-1 weight and size advantage over the average person. If the horse doesn't believe that you are in charge, it can and will dump you.

Prospects, parents, educators, and administrators are no different. Your emotions influence their emotions. If they sense fear, weakness, defensiveness, or lack of confidence, they will shut you down or bulldoze right over you. For this reason, when horses or people challenge you, no matter what emotions you are feeling, you must respond with a noncomplementary behavior—a behavior that counters and disrupts their pattern—*relaxed confidence.*

Emotions are contagious. When asking for what you want, relaxed confidence is the most persuasive nonverbal message. When you lack confidence in yourself, people tend to lack confidence in you. In most cases, they don't consciously understand why they feel the way they do. But things just don't feel right. This creates big problems when you are attempting to build trust with prospects (and their parents) and convince them to join the military.

If the enemy can sense your fear, you are a weak target. Prospects are the same. For this reason, you must develop and practice techniques for building and demonstrating relaxed confidence even when you feel the opposite so that on the outside you appear poised. For example, stepping out from behind your table at events and maintaining a confident, military bearing, even when you are uncomfortable.

This begins with controlling the message you are transmitting to prospects by managing your nonverbal communication including:

- Voice tone, inflection, pitch, and speed
- Body language and facial expressions

Table 6.1 lists which nonverbal communication conveys insecurity and which nonverbal communication conveys confidence.

Table 6.1   Comparison of Nonverbal Behaviors in Demonstrating Confidence

Demonstrates Lack of Confidence, Insecurity, and Fear	Demonstrates a Relaxed, Confident Demeanor
Speaking with a high-pitched voice.	Speaking with normal inflection and a deeper pitch.
Speaking fast. When you speak too fast, you sound untrustworthy.	Speaking at a relaxed pace with appropriate pauses.

(continued)

Table 6.1 (*continued*)

Demonstrates Lack of Confidence, Insecurity, and Fear	Demonstrates a Relaxed, Confident Demeanor
Tense or defensive tone of voice.	Friendly tone—a smile in your voice.
Speaking too loudly or too softly.	Appropriate voice modulation with emotional emphasis on the right words and phrases.
Frail or nervous tone of voice with too many filler words, "ums," "uhs," and awkward pauses.	Direct, properly paced tone and speech that gets right to the point.
Lack of eye contact—looking away. Nothing says "I can't be trusted" and "I'm not confident" like poor eye contact.	Direct, appropriate eye contact.
Hands in your pockets.	Hands by your side or out in front of you as you speak. Note: This may feel uncomfortable but it makes you look powerful and confident.
Wild gesticulations or hand motions.	Using hand gestures in a calm and controlled manner.
Touching your face or hair, or putting your fingers in your mouth—all clear signs that you are nervous or insecure.	Your hands in a power position—by your side or out in front of you in a controlled, nonthreatening manner.
Hunched over, head down, arms crossed.	Straight posture, chin up, shoulders straight and back. This posture will also make you feel more confident.

Table 6.1 (*continued*)

Demonstrates Lack of Confidence, Insecurity, and Fear	Demonstrates a Relaxed, Confident Demeanor
Shifting back and forth on your feet or rocking your body.	Standing still in a natural power pose.
Stiff posture, body tense.	Relaxed, natural posture.
Jaw clenched, tense look on face.	Relaxed smile. The smile is a universal language that says "I'm friendly and can be trusted."
Weak, limp, sweaty-palm handshake.	Firm, confident handshake delivered while making direct eye contact.

People are also subconsciously assessing the meaning of your words and assessing whether the words you use are congruent with your voice tone and body language. Confident messages increase the probability that you will get a *yes*. Whether you are communicating on the phone, in person, or via e-mail or social media, language matters—the words you use and how you structure those words convey loud and clear whether you are insecure, passive, and weak or confident and trustworthy (see Table 6.2).

Getting past the emotions that disrupt confidence is among the most formidable challenges for military recruiters. It's common to feel intimidated when meeting with educators and parents, have diminished confidence after experiencing a loss or failure, or become desperate when you are in danger of missing mission.

Even in emotionally draining situations, you must maintain the discipline to be aware of your emotions and how those emotions may be affecting other people. Self-awareness and self-control are like muscles. The more you exercise them, the stronger they get.

Table 6.2   Weak vs. Confident Messages

Nonassumptive, Passive, and Weak	Assumptive and Confident
"I'm just checking in."	"The reason I'm calling is . . ."
"I was wondering (hoping) if . . . ?"	"Tell me who—how—when—where—what . . ."
"I just wanted to reach out to see . . ."	"The purpose for my call is . . ."
"I have the whole day open."	"I'm super busy with interviews, but I have a slot available at 11:00 a.m."
"How does that sound?"	"Why don't we go ahead and get you in today for your ASVAB. How about right after school?"
"What's the best time for you?"	"I'll be visiting an applicant not far from you on Monday. I can pick you up for lunch."
"I kinda, sorta, was wondering if maybe you might have time to answer a few questions, if that would be okay?"	"Tell me about your plans after you graduate."
"Would this be a good time for you?"	"How about we meet again next Thursday at 2:00 p.m.?"
"I wanted to find out . . ."	"When can we speak with your parents?"
"How do you feel about this so far?"	"Based on everything you've told me about your current situation, I think it makes sense for us to move to the next step."

Table 6.2 (*continued*)

Nonassumptive, Passive, and Weak	Assumptive and Confident
"What do you think?"	"The next step is getting you scheduled and ready for MEPS."
"Do you have time now to take a practice test?"	"I recommend getting started with a short practice test to determine our next move."

Shut Up

The hardest part of asking is learning to ask and shut up. When you've asked for what you want, you've put it all out there and left yourself vulnerable to rejection.

What happens when you feel vulnerable? You try to protect yourself.

In that awkward moment after you ask, your head spins, your gut tightens, and rejection flashes before your eyes. The split second of silence is unbearable. It feels like an eternity. In this moment of weakness, you start talking, and talking, and talking—in the delusional belief that as long as you keep talking, the prospect can't reject you.

You attempt to deal with objections that have not even surfaced, introduce objections that didn't previously exist, overexplain yourself, offer your prospect a way out, and start blabbing on and on about MOS, benefits, your military experience, your dog, cat, kids, high school, or what you had for lunch. Eventually the prospect who was ready to say *yes* gets talked into saying *no*—by *you*. Your insecurity pushes them away.

After you ask you must *shut up*! Despite the alarm bells going off in your adrenaline-soaked brain, despite your pounding heart, sweaty palms, and fear, you must bite your tongue, sit on your hands, put the phone on mute, shut up, and allow your prospect to answer.

Be Prepared for Objections

Your ability to handle and get past objections is where the rubber meets the road in recruiting. It's where mission is made.

When you ask, you are going to get objections. It's an unassailable fact, and your brain knows it. This is why you anticipate and brace for rejection. It's why the mere seconds of silence between the ask and your prospect's response seem interminable.

When you are prepared to handle any objection that comes at you, though, you gain the confidence and courage to wait for your prospect to answer.

Later in this book, I'll give you the tools, techniques, and human influence frameworks you'll need to get past prospecting objections effectively and break through resistance to engage, qualify, and advance prospects and applicants through the recruiting pipeline.

PART III

On the Move

7

The More You Prospect, the Luckier You Get

Inaction breeds doubt and fear. Action breeds confidence and courage. If you want to conquer fear, do not sit home and think about it. Go out and get busy.
—Dale Carnegie, writer and lecturer

The unrelenting daily imperative for every military recruiter is keeping the funnel full of qualified prospects.

Ultra-high performers spend as much as 80 percent of their time on prospecting and qualifying activities for one important reason. A full applicant funnel means less stress and consistent mission contribution.

There are three core laws of prospecting that when heeded will ensure that you are moving a steady stream of new applicants into the funnel:

1. The Universal Law of Need
2. The 30-Day Rule
3. The Law of Replacement

In this chapter, we discuss the implications of these universal laws for success in recruiting. You will also learn why ignoring these laws causes recruiting slumps and how to get out of a slump if you find yourself in one.

> **Author Note:** Throughout this book I use the word *pipeline* (pipe) and *funnel* interchangeably to avoid using the same word over and over again. Most often, though, I use *pipeline* to describe prospects you are working to convert into applicants and *funnel* to describe applicants who are active and moving toward the floor—the Applicant Processing List (APL).

The Universal Law of Need

It is when funnels are empty that recruiters find themselves face to face with the *Universal Law of Need*. This law comes into play in recruiting when lack of prospecting activity has left your funnel depleted.

The Universal Law of Need states that the more you need the enlistment, the less likely it is that you will get it. When all of your hope for making mission rests on one, two, or even a handful of prospects or applicants, the probability that you will miss mission increases exponentially.

Consider Staff Sergeant Williams; her prospecting activity is inconsistent at best. Several applicants she was counting on were disqualified at MEPS. Because of this, she has only one applicant remaining in her funnel.

Now, with the end of the month (Phase Line) looming, Williams is under tremendous pressure to avoid a zero (and pulling contracts forward from the next PL). She desperately needs this applicant to enlist.

As she becomes more desperate, she comes face to face with a cruel reality: Desperation magnifies and accelerates failure and virtually guarantees the enlistment won't come through.

There are several reasons why desperation increases the probability that Williams will fail when she needs to succeed the most:

- The first is that desperation taps into the downside of the Law of Attraction, which states that what you focus your thoughts on, you are most likely to receive. When you are desperate, you no longer focus your thoughts on what is required for success. Instead, you focus on what will happen to you if you don't get what you need, thereby attracting failure.

- The next problem, because emotions are contagious, is other people can sense your desperation. Through your actions, tone of voice, words, and body language, you send the message that you are desperate and weak. That you lack confidence. Prospects and parents naturally repel recruiters who are needy and pathetic. When you reek of the foul stench of desperation, people don't enlist with you.

- Finally, when you are desperate, you become emotional and act illogically, which causes you to make poor decisions—like scratching lottery tickets by sending unqualified applicants to the floor; wasting time and energy endlessly seeking waivers for poorly qualified applicants; or wasting time in the delusional and desperate attempt to turn Cat-4s into Alphas. You may also make mistakes that can potentially ruin your career through investigation for recruiter misconduct and integrity violations.

In contrast to Williams, Sergeant First Class Santos is consistently prospecting, networking, gaining referrals, and systematically moving her applicants through the funnel. Her hard work has resulted in six Alphas and three Bravos in her funnel.

Will they all enlist? Maybe. However, Santos feels little pressure. She only needs to enlist one. Through her focus on daily prospecting, she is consistently replacing the applicants who fall out of her funnel. As a result, her productivity has been consistent and predictably on target.

She knows with confidence that she'll contribute to mission success and exactly how many enlistments she'll deliver tomorrow, next week, and next month. She has earned the trust of her command because she is dependable and consistently delivers.

Because her funnel is full, she exudes a relaxed and confident demeanor that allows her to attract and engage the highest qualified prospects. Santos gets a huge boost when she picks up an Alpha applicant through a referral—out of the blue. She didn't need this extra recruiting gravy, yet because she was disciplined in her activity, it fell right into her lap. The "Recruiting Gods" reward prospecting activity.

The 30-Day Rule

In military recruiting, the 30-Day Rule is always in play. The 30-Day Rule states that the prospecting you do in any given 30-day period will pay off over the next 90 days. It is a simple yet powerful universal rule that governs military recruiting—and you ignore it at your peril. When you embrace and internalize this rule, you will never again put prospecting aside for another day.

Sergeant Carter hit a bad slump. The previous quarter he'd exceeded mission and been the hero of his battalion. It was just his second quarter on the team. During his first three months in the field as a recruiter, he'd enthusiastically dived into prospecting, and it paid off. He scored seven enlistments.

But over the past couple of months, he'd allowed himself to get caught up in building packets, processing applicants, and handling admin work. He became complacent and stopped prospecting.

In his fifth month as a recruiter, Carter woke up to his second zero month, and his NCOIC in his face demanding that he get back on track. It was an up-front and close experience with the brutal reality that in recruiting it is not about who you *have* enlisted but rather who you enlist *today*.

When Carter reached out to me for help, he was in a precarious situation. His recruiting funnel was empty, and he felt like he was facing an uphill battle that he could never win. He justified his failure to prospect with all of the admin work he was required to do. He was sporting a piss-poor attitude and a ruck full of excuses. He complained that MEPS was the devil, the Army's qualification requirements were too stringent, his schools were against him, flighty teenagers wouldn't commit, and the helicopter parents were too afraid to let go.

I explained the 30-Day Rule and gave one clear and unambiguous order: "Quit whining and get on the phone and start dialing. Go get in your schools and out in the community and start talking to people."

To his credit, Carter took my advice and started prospecting—one call, one touch, one conversation at a time.

At first it didn't feel like he was making any progress—when you are desperate, you try to will the world to conform to your unreasonable deadlines. He felt that he was just going through the motions and sinking deeper into quicksand. He was working hard, doing the toughest work in recruiting, and still not getting enlistments.

But each day of calling and talking to potential recruits on the street and in his schools added opportunities to his pipeline. As he rebuilt his funnel, he rediscovered his confidence and sense of self-worth.

Carter stuck with it, and 90 days later he was once again the number-one recruiter in his company. The impact of daily prospecting on his performance— from zero to hero in just three months—made an indelible impression on Sergeant Carter. It was a lesson he never had to learn again.

The implication of the 30-Day Rule is simple. Miss a day of prospecting and it will tend to bite you sometime in the next

90 days. Miss a week and you're in jeopardy of missing mission. Blow off an entire month of prospecting, and Charlie Foxtrot. You tank your pipeline, roll a series of zeros, fall into a slump, and wake up 90 days later desperate, feeling like a loser, with no clue how you ended up there.

The Law of Replacement

Let's take a look at Master Sergeant Donald's recruiting pipeline. His write rate is 1:10 or ten percent. In other words, out of ten conducts, he contracts one.

> **Question:** If Donald has ten applicants in his funnel and enlists one, how many remain in his funnel?

When I ask this question in Fanatical Military Recruiting Bootcamps, most recruiters answer nine. But they are wrong.

The answer is: *zero.*

So how can $10 - 1 = 0$? Here's the math.

Based on his statistical conversion funnel, Donald has a probability of 1 in 10 of enlisting an applicant. The net result is that when he enlists one applicant, the other nine applicants are no longer viable. His applicant funnel will be reduced by ten. One enlisted, and the other nine will either back out, won't be granted a waiver, or will be disqualified at MEPS.

> **Replacement:** To keep his pipeline full, Donald must now replace those ten applicants with new opportunities.

The *Law of Replacement* can be a difficult concept to understand because it is a statistical formula. You may in fact argue against it, asking how we could *know* that the other nine applicants won't enlist. To make this argument, however, is missing the point. We are talking about statistical probabilities based on measurable conversion ratios. The stats tell us that over the long run, Master Sergeant Donald must replace those applicants to keep his recruiting funnel healthy and consistently make mission month in and month out.

The Law of Replacement is a critical concept to internalize, because failure to heed this law is the reason recruiters find themselves at the feast or famine amusement park riding on the desperation roller coaster. Up and down. Up and down. Constant stress. A hero one month, a total zero the next.

The lesson the Law of Replacement teaches is that you must constantly be pushing new applicants into your funnel so that you're replacing those who will naturally fall out. And you must do so at a rate that matches or exceeds your enlistment conversion ratio. This is the science of the recruiting funnel and the key to sustained, consistent success. It is why you must never, ever, ever stop prospecting.

The Anatomy of a Recruiting Slump

Ninety-nine percent of recruiting slumps can be linked directly to a failure to prospect. The anatomy of a recruiting slump looks something like this:

- At some point, you stopped prospecting (see the 30-Day Rule).
- Because you stopped prospecting, your pipeline stalls (see the Law of Replacement).
- You replace prospecting for *new* applicants with *chasing* the applicants in your funnel who have gone dark and wasting time with those who are unqualified.
- But those applicants are never going to enlist.
- You grow dependent on walk-ins, call-ins, and "hot" leads.
- You miss mission.

- As you experience this failure, your confidence erodes.
- Your crumbling confidence creates negative self-talk, and that further degrades your confidence, wrecks your enthusiasm, and causes you to feel like a loser.
- Feeling like a loser saps your energy and motivation for prospecting activity.
- Because you don't feel like prospecting, you double down— desperately calling the same dead-end applicants over and over. You get nowhere.
- The lack of prospecting activity makes your already stale pipeline even worse.
- You start hoping for silver bullets, scratching lottery tickets, and praying for a Cat-4 day to open. But because hope is not a strategy, nothing changes.
- You roll a zero.
- You sink deeper into your slump, get desperate, and then *bam!* You get slapped by the Universal Law of Need.
- You roll another zero.
- Your self-esteem and confidence take another hit.
- Your recruiting days become depressing black holes of stress, misery, and lame excuses.
- You'd rather be anywhere other than here.

Sooner or later, you will let down your guard and find yourself in desperate need of an enlistment. The cumulative impact of your poor decisions, procrastination, fear, lack of focus, and even laziness will have added up. Suddenly you find yourself in a slump and scrambling to make mission.

You can recover, but first you must acknowledge where the blame for your predicament lies. When you find yourself in a desperate situation, it's easy to fall back on human nature and blame everything and everyone for your plight except, of course, yourself.

The Universal Law of Need doesn't punish others, though. It punishes *you* for your failure to execute the daily disciplines required for success.

Oscar Mike: The First Rule of Recruiting Slumps

The first rule of holes is when you are in one, stop digging, and the first rule of recruiting slumps is when you are in one, get moving and start prospecting. The only real way to get out of a recruiting slump is to get back up to the plate and start swinging.

When you find yourself in a slump, take a breath, acknowledge that your negative emotions are just making things worse, and commit yourself to daily prospecting. Do whatever it takes to get your mind focused on prospecting and committing to daily goals. This begins with an honest look in the mirror and taking responsibility for your own culpability for the slump.

Don't spend a moment in thought about what might happen to you if you don't find qualified applicants. Worry won't change the future. Likewise, don't get mired down in regret over what you have failed to do. You cannot change the past.

Instead, put all your energy, emotion, and effort into actions that you control. Success in military recruiting is a simple equation of daily, weekly, monthly, quarterly, and annual activity. In other words, you are in complete control of your future. When you go back to the basics and focus on the right activity, the results will come. Be aware, though, that it will take at least 30 days of sustained and dedicated daily activity to get back on track.

Make Your Own Luck

One of my absolute favorite quotes comes from the late, great golfer Arnold Palmer: "The more I practice, the luckier I get."

There is a parallel in recruiting: *The more you prospect, the luckier you get.*

Will training, experience, and technique make you a better prospector? Of course. However, it is far more important that you prospect consistently than that you prospect using the best techniques. When you prospect consistently—and that means talking to new people every day—you will make mission.

The cumulative impact of daily prospecting is massive. You begin to connect with the right prospects, with the right message, at just the right time. Suddenly, referrals drop in your lap out of nowhere, Alphas and Prior Service start calling you, and Unicorns walk into your storefront looking for *you*. The Recruiting Gods reward you for your hard work. You get "lucky."

Most recruiters never get lucky though because they only do the minimum amount of prospecting required to just squeak by. And when they do start prospecting (usually out of desperation), they expect instant miracles. When those miracles don't happen, they gripe that prospecting doesn't work and crawl back into the warm comfort of mediocrity.

You can't expect to make prospecting calls for a single day and get miracles any more than you could expect to hit the driving range once and go on to win the US Open. It requires consistent commitment and discipline over time—a little bit every day.

So, go hit the phones, work your schools, initiate conversations with students, talk to strangers everywhere you go, canvass, send e-mails and text messages, ask for referrals, set up and work events, and leverage social media. Be fanatical. Don't let anything or anyone stop you.

The more you prospect, the luckier you get.

8

The Three Ps That Are Holding You Back

You cannot escape the responsibility of tomorrow by evading it today.
—Abraham Lincoln

Prospecting is interrupting. You don't enjoy being interrupted. Neither do your prospects. When you interrupt, the responses can be cold, harsh, and biting. Sometimes you face personal insults.

It's awkward to interrupt someone's day. You can't control their response, and this unknown leaves you feeling vulnerable. Anticipating their rejection causes fear and worry. Should your prospect react harshly to being interrupted, it can hurt. It's an uncomfortable affair that's emotionally easier to just avoid.

Frankly, in a perfect world military recruiters wouldn't have to interrupt prospects. It would be a loving utopia where recruiters and prospects sat in circles and sang "Kumbaya." In this world, qualified prospects would reach out and contact recruiters at just the right time, and no one would ever have to prospect again.

But that's a fantasy. In the War for Talent, if you wait for prospects to interrupt you, you will fail.

Prospecting has *always* been about the willingness on the part of the recruiter to interrupt. Relentless interrupting is fundamental to building robust recruiting pipelines. No matter your prospecting approach, if you don't interrupt relentlessly, your funnel will be anemic, and you will miss mission.

The number-one reason for failure in military recruiting is an empty funnel, and the number-one reason recruiters have empty funnels is their failure to prospect consistently.

Yet, in the face of this brutal and undeniable truth, most recruiters spend more time finding excuses not to prospect rather than just doing it. There are three mind-sets that hold recruiters back from talking to people and interrupting strangers:

1. Procrastination
2. Perfectionism
3. Paralysis

Procrastination

You've no doubt heard the children's riddle "What is the best way to eat an elephant?"

The answer, of course, is "One bite at a time."

It's a simple concept. But when it comes to the real world and real problems, it's not that easy.

Far too often we try to eat the elephants in our lives all in one bite, which results in stress, frustration, and failure. You can't do all of your prospecting for the month, or even a week, in a single day. It is impossible, and it will never get done. That's why it's not "prospecting day"; it's prospecting *every day*!

Yet recruiters put prospecting off—always with the promise that they'll "get around to it" tomorrow or later this week or Monday or whatever is the prevailing excuse of the day.

They delude themselves into believing that they can prospect once or twice a week and it will be okay.

And it's easy to put prospecting off because in recruiting you are removed from the flagpole. You are in a remote location. You create your own plans for the day—often based on vague "guidance" from your chain of command. You make decisions on how many attempts, when you'll make them, and through which channel.

Procrastination is an ugly disease that plagues the human race. No one is immune. You've got it, and I've got it. In fact, I have a PhD in procrastination—a bona fide expert. One year I bought a book called *How to Stop Procrastinating* (my New Year's resolution). That book sat unread on my bedside table for three years until I finally sold it at a garage sale.

Every major failure in my life has been a direct result of a collapse in my self-discipline to do the little things every day. Frankly, that's all failure really is. The cumulative impact of many poor decisions, slips in self-discipline, and things put off until it is too late. To add insult to injury, my failures were often accompanied by an embarrassing crescendo of desperate, hurried, and wasted activity trying to catch up and do it all at once, to save my hide.

It is in our nature as humans to procrastinate. It's easy to say, "Oh, I'm tired, I'll exercise tomorrow." It's easy to say, "I'll start my diet tomorrow, I'll quit smoking after this pack, I'll make up today's prospecting on Friday, I'll start reading that book next week"! It's in our nature to fool ourselves with these promises.

But there is no reward for procrastination. The failure to do the little things each day cripples your efforts to make mission. Lack of daily discipline results in mediocrity and failure.

To consistently deliver mission, you must develop the self-discipline to do a little bit of prospecting each day. You can't wait until the end of the week, end of the day, end of the month, or end of the quarter to prospect. You must prospect every day. Every day. Every day. A little bit *every day*.

Procrastinating is easy, but the cost is great. Many recruiters don't understand the price they have paid until they wake up one day and realize that they are staring down the barrel of an empty funnel, sitting on top of a big pile of should-a-dones, regret, and failure.

Procrastination is the grave in which mission is buried.

Perfectionism

I looked on as Petty Officer Second Class Schneider arranged his desk perfectly. Organized the prospecting list on his computer. Carefully researched each prospect on his list. Searched Google, searched Facebook, and reviewed in detail the history and call notes.

An hour went by. Then two. Finally, he made the first call—a call to a prospect on which he had done meticulous research. His call went to voice mail, as did the next call, and the next one. He sighed, "No one answers the phone these days."

After three calls, he stopped to get a cup of coffee, check e-mail, and arrange things on his desk again. Forty-five minutes later he packed up his things and headed out to visit his schools. In his quest for perfectionism, Schneider managed to make seven prospecting calls in about three hours, getting nothing in return for his effort.

Petty Officer First Class Lord has a desk right next to Schneider's. As soon as she sat down at her desk that same morning, she pulled a prospecting list and started dialing. An hour later she'd made 33 calls, spoken to 14 people, and set up two interviews with qualified prospects. Then she sent a dozen text messages to the numbers that didn't have voice mail set up and sent 19 e-mails to prior service prospects she was attempting to engage.

It wasn't perfect. She ran into a few snags, had a couple of calls that might have gone better had she researched in advance, and got a few harsh objections. However, she accomplished far more than Schneider. Lord is a top ten recruiter in her region.

In her *Huffington Post* article "14 Signs Your Perfectionism Has Gotten Out of Control," Carolyn Gregoire writes, "The great irony of perfectionism is that while it's characterized by an intense drive to succeed, it can be the very thing that prevents success.

Perfectionism is highly correlated with fear of failure (which is generally not the best motivator) and self-defeating behavior, such as excessive procrastination."[1]

This statement describes perfectly why perfectionism is the archenemy of prospecting. It generates both procrastination and the fear of rejection. The late motivational speaker Zig Ziglar said, "Anything worth doing is worth doing poorly."

I've always believed that messy success (moving and taking action) is far better than perfect mediocrity (waiting until the "perfect" moment).

I'll beat the recruiter who spends a call block meticulously researching each prospect on any day by just picking up a targeted list and calling. Sure, I'll miss a few things here and there if I don't read every note and know everything, but there won't be enough of a delta to compensate for the activity gap between me and the recruiter who gets everything perfect before making a single prospecting call.

To be clear, I am not saying that researching or organizing your prospecting block is a bad idea. If you are calling high-potential prospects, it is a good idea to research in advance so that you can make the message relevant to their unique situation and engage them in a conversation.

Advance is the optimal word, though. *Research is not prospecting.* Do research *before* and *after* the Golden Hours (or Red Time) so that it does not encroach on your prospecting activity and productivity.

When you delude yourself into believing that research is prospecting, then perfect research, perfect organization, finding the perfect time to call, or having the perfect situation to talk to a prospect becomes an obsession that you use to shield yourself from potential rejection.

Most of the problem with perfectionism is self-talk. The voice inside your head tells you that when you get all of your little ducks in a perfect row, prospects will be putty in your hands. This self-talk manifests itself in behaviors that have you working hard to get everything ready and perfect but not actually doing anything. You plan to plan to plan to plan but accomplish nothing.

The solution is simple. Block time for prospecting. Set a goal for the number of touches you will make during that time block. Then do it.

Paralysis from Analysis

Talking to strangers conjures up our deepest, darkest fear—being rejected. The truth is we are all reluctant to call and talk to strangers. It's not normal for human beings to seek out rejection, yet that is exactly what you are asked to do as a recruiter.

For this reason, humans tend to anticipate rejection, which manifests itself in the form of worry that creates paralysis from analysis. This problem is driven in part by perfectionism and is totally fixable. Here is what analysis paralysis sounds like emanating from the mouths of military recruiters:

> "Well, what if they say no?"
> "What if their parents say no?"
> "What if they say this or that?"
> "How will I know if . . . ?"
> "What should I do if . . . ?"
> "What should I say if . . .?"
> "What if I bring them in for an interview and they are not qualified?"

Rather than just dialing the phone, initiating a conversation in line at Target, or walking through their front door and dealing with what comes next, recruiters, driven by fear and worry, go on a "what if" binge, often followed by an attempt to get every duck in a perfect row. The result: Prospecting grinds to a halt.

Disrupting the Three Ps

When working with recruiters who are held back by one or all of the Three Ps, I get them focused on making just one prospecting call.

Then the next. Then the next. One call at a time. Sometimes I get a list and sit next to them and dial, too. When they see that I'm not getting blown out of the water by prospects, it gets easier for them to let go of these mental hang-ups and disruptive emotions and take action.

Sometimes I must be direct to get them to jump into prospecting. I push them hard to "just do it." Just pick up the phone and make the call. Let the "what ifs" take care of themselves. This is how we do it in our Fanatical Military Recruiting Boot Camps. We give the order, "You've got 15 minutes to make 15 calls and set one appointment. *Go!*"

No time to think, no time to plan, no time to worry. Just pick up the phone and dial. I know this might seem harsh, but a push is sometimes what's required to break this destructive cycle. It's not much different from how I learned to swim or how you learned to be a Soldier, Marine, Airman, or Sailor.

I was six and shivering. My toes hung precariously off the edge of the diving board that jutted out over the lake at Athens Y Camp in north Georgia. The hulking six-foot-five frame of Coach Poss, the waterfront director, towered over me.

We'd spent the last five days learning strokes, how to kick, and how to breathe, all in the safety of the shallow end. Now it was the moment of truth. Each student had to jump from the diving board into the dark, cold, deep lake and swim the ten feet or so to shore. It seemed like a mile to me.

I looked back at Coach Poss. "What if I can't swim? What if I don't come back up? Can I please do it tomorrow?" I pleaded. I stood on the end of that diving board staring at the water, running over all of the worst-case scenarios in my head.

Coach Poss began walking toward me. He was neither amused nor swayed by my begging for more time. There was only one thing I feared more than jumping into the lake, and he was getting closer by the second. He'd already unceremoniously hurled a couple of reluctant beginner swimmers from the diving board. I did not want that embarrassment, so I jumped.

I hit the cold water and went under. For a moment, I panicked. Then I stroked my arms and kicked my feet and burst through the surface. I remembered my lessons and paddled my way to the shore. The strokes were not perfect—more dog paddle than breast stroke—but I made it. I made it!

After that, you couldn't keep me off that diving board. Coach Poss taught me to swim because he forced me to do it. He wasn't worried. He knew I wouldn't drown.

We've all found ourselves in the crushing grip of the insidious Three Ps. I observe recruiters endlessly obsessing and overthinking the potential outcomes of prospecting calls. They convince themselves that they need to gather more facts, just need a little bit more training, or that the timing is not right. They squander time worrying about what ifs and look at me with puppy dog eyes pleading for more time to get it right before diving in.

Think back to when you were at boot camp. You were asked to do and experience things that were foreign to you. At times you were afraid or hesitant. But your drill sergeant pushed you to do the things you thought you could not do. It's been like this throughout your career in the military. You've faced adversity and succeeded. Through repetition, you gained obstacle immunity and resilience.

The human mind abhors the unknown. In its natural state, it wants to be safe and secure. It doesn't like leaping off a diving board into a cold lake, jumping out of a plane, running into live fire, rappelling down a wall, or picking up a phone and calling a stranger (especially a teenager). It panics in the face of change and clings to the status quo. Then it begins to convince us that all kinds of awful dire consequences are imminent.

But at some point, you've got to move. Sometimes you just need a Coach Poss or a drill sergeant or a Coach Jeb to push you to take action.

PART
IV
Battle Rhythm

9

Time Discipline

One of the best ways to keep peace is to be prepared for war.
—General George Washington

The greatest threat to mission is not lack of training, lack of talent, poor attitude, society, politics, generational differences, the news cycle, or any of the things that are often blamed for mission failure.

No, the most formidable threat to mission is where, how, and with whom recruiters choose to invest their time. When your behavior is shaped and driven by paralysis, perfectionism, and procrastination, you make very poor choices with the limited amount of time you have for recruiting.

At the beginning of every Fanatical Military Recruiting training program, we ask participants to tell us their greatest recruiting challenge. Eighty percent of the recruiters and recruiting leaders who attend our sessions say that they struggle most with having enough time to recruit.

The constant refrain: "I just never seem to have enough time for prospecting with everything else I have to get done."

There is no doubt that most military recruiters are working insanely long hours. Which strains and disrupts relationships with their spouses and families and it impacts quality of life and work-life balance. Yet for recruiters, most time management problems are self-inflicted.

- Yes, recruiters and recruiting leaders have more on their plate each day than can ever be accomplished.
- Yes, military branches are asking more of their recruiters and leaders than ever before.
- Yes, the bureaucracy can be a nightmare to navigate.
- Yes, there are packets to create, waivers to process, e-mail to return, calls and information to record in the Recruiting Information Support System (RISS), meetings and training to attend, PT, conference calls, drills, and asses to kiss.

However, while military recruiting is not, and never will be, a 9 to 5 job, a well-organized and disciplined recruiter can consistently make mission *and* have a balanced life at home.

The difference between ultra-high performers and stressed-out recruiters who miss mission and can't understand "how the UHPs can possibly get it all done" is that ultra-high performers are masters at maximizing prime recruiting time (the Golden Hours/Red Time) for . . . *recruiting*.

Twenty-Four

The one constant for every recruiter is time—time for prospecting, time for interviews, time for school and community events, time for packet building, time for parental meetings, time for follow-up, time for MEPS visits, and time for administrative tasks, data entry, and paperwork.

Motivational speaker Dennis Waitley wrote that "time is an equal opportunity employer. Each human being has exactly the same number of hours and minutes every day. Rich people can't buy more hours. Scientists can't invent new minutes. And you can't save time to spend it on another day. Even so, time is amazingly fair and forgiving. No matter how much time you've wasted in the past, you still have an entire tomorrow."

Time is not a renewable resource. You cannot make more, add more, or find more time. Every recruiter has exactly 24 hours each day. No more.

Only a third, or so, of your 24 hours each day are available for recruiting activities. It's how efficiently and effectively you use these "Golden Hours" that is the ultimate difference between failure, average, and ultra-high performance. When you master time, territory, and resource management, you'll lower your stress level, make mission faster and more consistently, and have more time to spend with your family and on other things you enjoy.

My primary objective with this chapter is to slap you in the face with the cold hard truth of how you hold yourself back with the choices you make with your time. I want to evoke acute awareness of how critical time discipline is to your success in military recruiting.

My goal is to shift your mind-set about how you schedule and manage time for prospecting and other recruiting activities. I want you to take an honest look at:

- the consequences of the choices you are making now about time,
- how you allow distractions to waste prime recruiting time,
- how the Three Ps cause you to be delusional about the best use of time,
- how the cumulative impact of small slips in time discipline is negatively impacting mission and the rest of your life.

Let's begin with another immutable truth: You cannot manage time. Time is inextricable and relentless. You cannot stop it, get it back, reinvest it, or recover it. Once it is gone, it is *gone*. Time is by nature unmanageable. What is manageable is *you*—the way you think about time and the choices you make about time.

Time discipline is a simple choice between what you want *now* and what you want *most*.

Let's keep this real. For your entire time in the military, someone else has set your routine and managed your time. There was a time to wake, a time for chow, a time to drill, a time for PT, a time for training, a time to sleep, a time for deployment, and a time for R&R. Those were much simpler days.

Consider General Lewis B. "Chesty" Puller's humorous reply to a Marine's formal request for permission to be married: "Son, if the Marines thought you needed a wife, we would have issued you one." For your entire military career, someone else did the thinking for you. You showed up when you were told to show up and did what you were told to do. Life revolved around the flagpole.

Then your tour of duty as a military recruiter began. In this MOS, you were handed the keys to a government vehicle, a phone, a box of business cards, a laptop, and a number (mission). You were told to go figure it out. Suddenly you had both the freedom and the responsibility to choose how you use your time.

In the civilian world, we say that time is money. *In military recruiting, time is mission.*

Leveraging Horstman's Corollary

The NCOIC was desperate for a solution. His recruiting team was behind on mission, and things were not getting better.

I spent a day observing his recruiting team paint the grass. Heads stuck in laptops, shuffling paper, sending e-mails, hanging out on Facebook, whining, complaining, and planning to plan to plan to recruit. The recruiting floor was silent.

The activity data from the previous 90 days told the story. On average, each recruiter was making less than a third of the prospecting touches and interviews required to make mission. It was shocking. These recruiters, whose job it was to talk to prospects, were talking to no one except themselves.

When I finally pulled the team together and confronted them with the numbers, there were excuses—lots of excuses. "You don't understand, Jeb! We've got so many other things to do—meetings, following up, packets, admin work, waivers, e-mail. It's impossible to find quality candidates, no one can pass the test, the parents won't let us talk to their sons and daughters, and we can't get into schools."

The excuses continued. "MEPS is worse than ever: They're kicking everyone back for eyes, ears, psych, the 'flavor of the month'," etc. The Recruiting Information Support System is clunky, the coffee is decaffeinated, the military bureaucracy is in the way, people don't answer their phones in the morning, afternoon, Wednesdays, or during full moons . . ."

I loved that one. *No one answers the phone.* They were not amused when I pointed out that nobody answers a phone *that doesn't ring.* Been there, done that, got the T-shirt and the tattoo. I'd heard it all before—every lame excuse for doing anything other than interrupting prospects and pulling them into the recruiting funnel.

So I pointed out that the funnel was *empty.* They were barely contributing any enlistments to the battalion's mission, and those they were contributing were random prospects who walked in off of the street and interrupted *them.*

I was incredulous. "How in the world can you be spending so much time on follow-up calls and building packets when, essentially, there are no applicants in the funnel?" I asked.

They stared back at me. The room got cold. Crickets. The truth hit them like a brick right to the middle of the forehead. The entire team was living in the land of delusion. Before they could launch into more excuses, I made them each pull together a list of 50 prospects.

Ten minutes later, with lists in their hands, I gave them 30 minutes to call 25 prospects and set two interviews. Do not pass go, do not collect $200, do not watch cat videos, no Facebook, no e-mail. Pen, list, phone. Dial!

There were stunned looks on their faces. They fidgeted in their seats and stared at their phones. Two recruiters said they felt more comfortable calling in a quieter place. One started down the road of how now "was a bad time to call" (which seems to always be the case with *now*).

I wasn't budging. No excuses were sticking. Teflon. No more BS. No more putting it off. As Benjamin Franklin said, you may delay, but time will not. So, with me standing there unmoving and impervious to their excuses, the recruiters got down to work.

Thirty minutes later, on average, each recruiter had made seventeen attempts and set at least one appointment for an interview. They made more attempts and set more interviews in just thirty minutes than they had in the previous two weeks combined.

I had their attention. The recruiters were shaking their heads, saying that they couldn't believe how many people answered the phone. The NCOIC was blown away by how much the team had accomplished in such a short period of time.

All I had done was leverage the *Horstman's Corollary to Parkinson's Law*.

Parkinson's Law states that work tends to expand to fill the time allotted for it. Give someone eight hours to do something that takes an hour—like make 50 prospecting attempts—and it will take the entire eight hours. Horstman's Corollary is the converse. It describes how work contracts to fit into the time allowed. I simply changed the paradigm the recruiters were working under—instead of giving them an entire day to make their prospecting calls, I gave them 30 minutes.

I repeat this exercise with recruiters within every branch of the military—in small and large groups—and the results are always the same. Recruiters and leaders are absolutely stunned at how much they get done when they block their time, focus on a single activity, and set a goal for the outcome of that activity.

Time Blocking

Ultra-high performers organize their days into distinct time blocks dedicated to specific activities, concentrating their focus on a single activity and eliminating distractions within those blocks.

They develop recruiting territory plans that minimize drive time. In the office, they block time for and prioritize prospecting activity. They also block out time for building packets, following up, managing waiver requests, and planning events, in-school work, and every other part of their day. They are flexible, adaptive, and creative in their quest to maximize their use of time for recruiting and minimize any distraction that takes away from moving applicants into and through the pipeline.

Time blocking is transformational for recruiters. It changes everything. You become incredibly efficient when you block your day into short chunks of time for specific activities. You get more accomplished in a shorter time with far better results.

Time blocking is the foundation of your *daily battle rhythm* (DBR) and recruiting routine. When you get disciplined at blocking your time and concentrating your focus on a single activity in each time block with no other distractions, there is a massive and profound impact on your productivity.

For example, the average inside sales rep at my company—Sales Gravy—makes 120 outbound prospecting calls a day selling employment advertising. To most people, this seems like an impossible number of calls. But what really causes a double take is when they learn that we do this in just three hours—which leaves plenty of time for all of the other selling activities we need to do.

We schedule our prospecting blocks into three "Power Hours" that are spread across the day—morning, midday, and afternoon. We break our power hours up into *high-intensity prospecting sprints* (HIPS)—10-, 15-, 20-, or 30-minute blocks, depending on the day.

During Power Hours we do nothing but make calls. We remove all distractions. We don't do research, allow ourselves to get sucked into e-mail or admin tasks, drift off into the internet or social media sites, or accept any excuses. We don't take breaks to get coffee or go to the restroom.

We minimize the downtime between calls by having our targeted call lists prepared and researched in advance. We take notes during the block and wait until after the block concludes to log our calls and update the contact records—during time that is blocked specifically for updating activity. We also schedule blocks for e-mail, text messaging, and social prospecting.

Don't get me wrong. It is intense, draining, rejection-dense work. We make targeted calls (we are not just going through the motions) as fast as possible, minimizing time between each attempt. Power Hours work brilliantly for two reasons:

1. The hard work of prospecting contracts into the time allotted for it, so we get more done in less time.
2. It's much easier to remain focused during these short HIPS.

The good news is most recruiters can keep their funnels full of qualified applicants with just a few hours a day of prospecting when that activity is consistent, done every day, and concentrated into set prospecting blocks.

When you block time for prospecting, concentrating your focus inside high-intensity sprints, along with making prospecting an integral part of your DBR, I absolutely and unequivocally guarantee that in less than 90 days, your pipeline will be packed, and you will *make mission fast!*

Stick to Your Guns and Avoid Distractions

Let's suppose that you had an appointment set with an Alpha prospect and his parents. It had taken two months to get the appointment. They are expecting you to be at their home at 18:30. As you are getting ready to walk out of the door for the meeting, one of your fellow recruiters comes by your desk, to say he's going out to get pizza. He wants to know if you want to go.

Would you? Would you just walk out the door and blow off that meeting? Of course not! That would be completely irresponsible and stupid. You would tell your peer that you had an important appointment and that you couldn't go.

Prospecting blocks should be scheduled or "blocked" on your calendar with the same level of commitment. You must treat them as if they are sacred—in the same way you view a set meeting with your boss, a parent, an applicant, an administrator, or an important event with your family.

Because prospecting is difficult, rejection-dense work, it's easy to find anything to do other than interrupt strangers. Because you are constantly battling the gravitational pull of the Three Ps, you will always find convenient excuses for not prospecting. This is why, when it comes to time blocking and your DBR, you must stick to your guns.

Let nothing or no one—not even yourself—interfere with or steal that time. Many recruiters who have gone through our courses hang signs on their doors or place them on their desks to warn others to leave them alone during their phone blocks.

It is discipline, pure and simple. You, above all others, must hold yourself accountable to schedule your prospecting blocks and keep them sacred. No one else can make that decision—only you.

Concentrate Your Focus

Time blocking makes you so productive because it forces you to concentrate intensely on a single focus. Of course, this flies right in the face of a culture that has elevated multitasking to mythical status.

Perhaps you are the kind of person who believes you can multitask. You can field text messages from your mom, scan your Facebook feed, take calls from applicants, answer e-mails, update the Recruiting Information Support System, and research each prospect, all while you are making prospecting calls. You pride yourself on being a multitasker and even brag about your ability to do many things at the same time.

Here's the truth: *You suck at it.*

Basic neuroscience refutes the delusional human belief that we are good at multitasking. Our brains *can't* multitask. Instead, when you are working on more than one thing at a time, your brain cycles back and forth between those things. It does this so rapidly that you have the *illusion* of multitasking—even though you are not actually multitasking.

Your brain was not made to multitask. Sure, it was designed to operate in complex environments and process multiple streams of data at once. You can cook dinner and watch TV at the same time. You can drive and talk. But your brain was not made to talk, walk, rub your belly, and chew gum simultaneously. You simply cannot do multiple tasks all at one time and do them well. And here's the kicker. Each time your brain shifts from one task to the other, that shift causes you to move slower and lose efficiency.

When you have too many things going on at once (especially complex tasks), your brain bogs down, and you slow down. This is called cognitive overload. It is no different from what happens when you have too many complex programs running at the same time on your computer. At some point, the processor can't handle the load and runs slower and slower.

Be honest. You know you've banged into another person or almost been mowed down by a bus while you were staring at your phone screen and texting. You know you've escaped death more than once while talking on the phone, checking e-mail, or texting while you were driving your car.

Most recruiters I work with believe that they *should* be multitasking. They make a call, log it into their RISS, research the next prospect through a web search or social media query, answer an e-mail from the boss, take calls, monitor social media streams, send a prospecting e-mail, send text messages, build packets, follow up on applicants, chase waivers, and instant message their peers.

When I point out that with all of this going on, it took them an hour to make four prospecting calls, they stare back in disbelief. "No," they'll explain, "I made way more than that." Delusion brought on by multitasking.

Here's another truth: Prospecting efficiency decreases in direct proportion to the number of things you are attempting to do at one time. You spend five to ten minutes per prospecting touch because you've got so many other things going.

Recently I was working with a team of recruiters who were averaging seven telephone prospecting dials during a one-hour phone block. That's eight and a half minutes per attempt. It wasn't like they were sitting around doing nothing. They were busy, busy, busy multitasking. Yet they weren't making a dent in mission.

After a short time together, during which we turned every distraction off and focused on prospecting, they averaged 36 dials an hour. What changed? It was a simple concentration of focus. Rather than diluting their focus by trying to do multiple tasks at one time, they concentrated on only one—*dial the phone*.

- Mobile devices were turned off and placed into drawers.
- E-mail was turned off.
- Signs were placed on doors alerting others that they were in a phone block.

- Research was done and call objectives set before the phone block.
- Instead of logging the result of each call into the Recruiting Information Support System at the time of the call, we created lists in advance and made notes on the list. Then we blocked 30 minutes after the call block to log everything into the RISS.

The result was both efficiency and effectiveness. Performance improved exponentially—more prospects were qualified, and more interviews were set.

With all their phone attempts knocked out in just an hour, they could shift their focus to other blocks, like social prospecting, text messaging, packet building, outbound e-mail prospecting, interview prep, and follow-up calls.

Beware of the Ding

Petty Officer Second Class Lewis abandoned the prospecting call she was about to make, looked down, and reached for her phone. The sound it had made compelled her to check it. Two text messages, a Facebook post, and a YouTube video (which she texted to a friend) later, she finally shifted her attention back to her prospecting list but couldn't remember where she'd left off. Seven minutes had gone by since she'd looked down at her phone. She was oblivious.

Over the course of two hours, her attention shifted and she lost her focus 17 times. When e-mails came in, her computer would go ding, and she'd stop and look at each one—sometimes for just a moment, but twice she stopped completely to fret and respond.

When her two-hour prospecting block ended, she'd achieved just a fraction of her activity target. Then (I can't make this stuff up) she turned to me and said, "See, these mission targets they give us are ridiculously unreasonable. There is no way anybody can possibly accomplish what they are asking us to do. There isn't nearly enough time in the day."

The four biggest culprits derailing recruiters from prospecting are:

- E-mail
- Mobile devices
- Social media and the internet
- Peers

When something new hits your in-box or social stream—ding, buzz, lights, action!—like clockwork, your attention shifts to e-mail or a smartphone. Twenty minutes later, you find yourself watching a video of a chimpanzee riding a giraffe around a circus tent and can't remember how you got there. When another recruiter stops by your desk to tell a joke, complain, or chat you up, it's the perfect excuse to abandon the hard work of prospecting.

Mobile devices are the worst offenders, though. They are addictive and intrusive. Two thousand, six hundred seventeen times as day.[1] That's how many times the average person looks at their phone screen. Look down—ding—and just like that, you get sucked in. Even as I write this paragraph, my iPhone is calling to me. I put it another room so I'd stay focused on my writing block, but I miss it!

You cannot be efficient or effective when you are constantly being distracted. Besides losing time to the distraction itself, you lose time trying to remember where you left off before you were distracted. This is why time blocking and concentrating your focus inside those blocks makes you so much more productive and is transformational for recruiters.

This means that during prospecting blocks, or building packet blocks, or follow-up call blocks, or whatever block you are in, you need to turn everything else *off*. Schedule alternate time blocks for dealing with e-mail, watching cat videos, or hanging out on Facebook.

What Lurks in Your In-box Can and Will Derail Your Recruiting Day

E-mail is the great time-sucker of the twenty-first century. It is an always-on stream of consciousness. It follows you everywhere (on your phone, tablet, laptop) and demands your attention.

E-mail is the derailer of all derailers. The time-sucker of all time-suckers. If you are itching for a few unproductive hours that you will never get back, just open up e-mail and dive in.

In our always-on society, e-mail has become an addiction. We feel compelled to check it, file it, manage it, rate it, flag it, spam it, and respond to it immediately. We delude ourselves into believing that if we don't jump right on it, we'll be judged as nonresponsive or worse. This is why it has a tendency to take priority over everything else.

Consider this: When you are with an applicant's parents sitting in their living room, do you interrupt them by saying, "Hey, could you hold a second? I just got an e-mail. It's nonsense, but I should answer."

Do you leave your phone or laptop sitting on their coffee table dinging and beeping while you are in the middle of a recruiting conversation? Sound ridiculous?

Yet you'll interrupt a prospecting block to answer trivial e-mails that can easily wait for an hour—or forever—to be answered.

If you were to get up early with me, grab a cup of coffee, and sit in recruiting offices observing recruiters in the wild, you'd see recruiters walk through the door in the morning, sit down at their desk, take a sip of coffee, and dive headlong into e-mail.

Whenever you open e-mail first thing in the morning, there is almost never good news. That Alpha you've been pursuing for months didn't suddenly come to her senses at 2:00 a.m. and send you a note telling you that she's ready.

Nope. You've got four messages from your boss giving you nonrecruiting busy work to do; an e-mail telling you that you haven't completed the compulsory compliance training; a handful of denied waivers; and 72 CYA, FYI, BTW, and OMG e-mails that require no action. But you feel compelled to respond immediately to all of them, just to prove that you are still breathing.

It's also the perfect excuse to avoid the hard work of prospecting.

When you start your day on e-mail, it's like stepping into glue. It slows you down, saps your energy, and wastes a massive amount of time. And once you are in your in-box, it is very, very difficult to climb out and focus on prospecting.

"But Jeb, what if one of the e-mails is important? What should I do then?" This is one of my favorite whines from recruiters who are unwilling to face the truth about e-mail. Of course, some e-mails are going to be important. But important does not mean urgent. You will rarely get an urgent e-mail first thing in the morning, and if you do and don't respond, they'll call or text you.

Take care of your prospecting block, then manage e-mail. Mission comes first.

Blocking out the first one to two hours of each day for focused prospecting is the mark of fanatical military recruiters. Depending on the time of year, you can easily reach and connect with students, graduates, and prior service first thing in the morning. When you start your day with prospecting, it gives you momentum to attack the rest of the day with confidence.

Driving Is Not an Accomplishment

You start on one side of your territory to visit a school, then drive an hour in the other direction to another. You give no thought to that wasted hour because driving, moving, going to the next stop feels like work.

But it's not work. It's not recruiting. It is delusion. Driving is not an accomplishment. The greatest waste of time for military recruiters is staring at a windshield.

Ultra-high performers minimize drive time by segmenting their territory into small pieces—by zip codes, school zones, cities, counties—and breaking their territory up by day of the week (or month when working in large rural territories). They group appointments, interviews, and activities inside of those segments and days. And, they get in as many prospecting touches as possible by doing area canvasing around school visits and appointments and prospecting while filling up the gas tank, getting food, waiting in line, and so on.

Be intentional about scheduling your day and when and where you set appointments and interviews. Minimize the time you spend driving and maximize time you spend talking to prospects. Squeeze every drop of value from the Golden Hours.

Protect the Golden Hours

Each moment of the recruiting day, you are faced with decisions about how to invest your time. And each moment you have three choices:

1. Spend your time on things that are *trivial* and add little value.
2. Spend your time on *important* things, like building packets, following up with applicants, submitting waivers, and fulfilling other admin and job requirements.
3. Spend your time on activities that are *impactful*. The most impactful thing you can do as a recruiter is prospecting to move qualified applicants into the recruiting funnel.

The Law of Triviality (an offshoot of Parkinson's Law) describes the human tendency to waste time on unimportant activities while mission-critical tasks are ignored. When humans are given a list of things to do, they almost always gravitate toward the trivial.

It's why so many recruiters waste time on nonrecruiting activities and make that an excuse for their failure to make mission. It's not uncommon for recruiters to waste 50 percent or more of their time on low-value activities. Now, don't misunderstand. You must do the *important* things. If you don't, applicants won't get to the floor, and you'll have a pissed-off boss up your rear. There is a bureaucracy to feed.

The single biggest challenge for recruiters, though, is keeping activities that don't generate mission from interfering with the Golden Hours. It's a challenge for many reasons:

- There will always be people making nonrecruiting requests that require your attention.
- When your prospecting activity levels are high, you will naturally generate more interviews, follow-up tasks, packets, waivers, data entry, and MEPS briefings and visits.
- Doing nonrecruiting activity feels important—like you are getting things done.
- Nonrecruiting activity is the perfect excuse to avoid the hard work of prospecting and face-to-face interviews. This is the core reason recruiters dig holes for themselves. Busy work becomes an excuse for not recruiting.

Let me make this crystal clear. Recruiters get paid to recruit—to make mission, fast. Period. Your core focus is simple:

1. Get prospects into the funnel.
2. Move applicants through the funnel.
3. Generate enlistments.

One, two, three. End of story. This is how you make an *impact*. Whine and complain about all the stuff you've got to do if you like, but whining will not change the fact that your job is to interact with qualified prospects during the Golden Hours and move them into and through the recruiting funnel.

Therefore, if you are not doing things that are not directly related to recruiting during the Golden Hours, then you are not doing your job. I've heard the same BS excuses a million times:

> *Wait a minute, Jeb, what about all of those things I'm asked to do by my leaders and the military? When am I supposed to get it all done?*
>
> *If "they" didn't put so much on me, I might have time to actually recruit [eyes rolling—sarcastic tone].*
>
> *What about my work-life balance? I've got a family, dog, golf game, friends, stuff I've got to do!*

Here are your choices:

- **Prioritize.** Get your priorities straight. Not everything is a priority, and in some cases, this means that some tasks may not get done. That's okay. Keep the funnel full and consistently accomplish mission, and no one will ever remember.
- **Front-load your day with impact:** It's easy to start your day with the trivial and important and think you'll save the impactful activities for later. But because impactful activities are often difficult, they tend to get pushed off to another day. The key then is to block your day so it is front-loaded with impact, then move to important, and save the trivial for later—or better yet, never.
- **Be more efficient.** Stop wasting your time on trivial distractions. Block your time for prospecting, processing, and the other activities that are part of the recruiting day. Concentrate your focus and effort on high-value activities. When you do, you'll accomplish far more, in less time, with greater outcomes.
- **Just say no.** One of the most effective ways to unload nonrecruiting activity is to just say no, respectfully. You don't have to take on or do everything that others bring to you. Whenever someone brings a task to you that is not mission critical and

could derail your Golden Hours—say no. Because you are in the military, this won't be easy. Respectful, tactful, and assertive are the names of the game. However, if you consistently create reasonable boundaries, it won't take long for others to get the message—especially when you are performing at a high level.

- **Delude yourself.** You can continue along the same track, deluding yourself that doing busy work during the Golden Hours is actual recruiting work. However, you cannot be delusional and make mission at the same time.

Leverage the Platinum Hours

In recruiting, time is mission and mission is accomplished in the Golden Hours. To make mission, you will have to make some sacrifices. You'll need to schedule nonrecruiting activities before and after the normal recruiting day, sometimes even on weekends.

To maximize recruiting productivity and make mission fast, your total focus must be on prospecting, qualifying, interviewing, and getting applicants to the floor. That, of course, means that a number of tasks must wait until before or after the Golden Hours. These periods are the Platinum Hours.

There will always be important nonrecruiting activities that you must do to be successful in your job. Do these things before and after prime recruiting time—in the Platinum Hours. Ultra-high-performing recruiters set aside time early each morning or late each afternoon to attack important nonrecruiting activities either before the demands of the recruiting day kick in or after they've been addressed.

UHPs use the Platinum Hours for:

- Building prospecting lists
- Research
- Interview planning
- Building packets

- Dealing with the bureaucracy
- Asking for waivers
- Social recruiting activities
- E-mail prospecting
- Prospect research
- Planning and organization
- Administration and reports
- Responding to e-mails
- Calendar management
- Recruiting Information Support System (RISS) management

During the Platinum Hours, you set up your day so you can focus on one thing: *high-impact activities that fill the funnel and contribute to mission.*

Adopt a Command Mind-Set

Time discipline is about the choices you make. The bottom line is you've got roughly eight Golden Hours each day to make mission, and you have a choice to either:

- Dawdle those hours away, whining that "they" give you too much paperwork, there's too much reporting, admin, traffic, bad prospects, or whatever lame excuse you are using that day to justify the fact that you are wasting time.
- Adopt a *command mind-set* and plan effectively, segment your territory, block your time, front-load your day with impact, remove distractions, and stick to your guns when others try to corrupt, interrupt, or usurp your time for their use.

The command mind-set is the most critical component of time, territory, and resource management. Unless and until you are willing to accept complete responsibility for owning your time, nothing will change. When you adopt a command mind-set, you choose to see yourself as the commander of *you. You* choose to *own it.*

Commanders are tasked with achieving objectives by leveraging the scarce resources available to them—people, time, and assets. They bear the ultimate responsibility for the results of their organization. They cannot push blame off on anyone else. They are expected to deliver on promises and achieve their objectives. The buck stops with them.

Fanatical military recruiters adopt a *command mind-set.*

- They believe that they and they alone are accountable for their own success or failure. They take complete responsibility for and ownership of managing their time, territory, schools, prospect pipeline, applicant funnel, mission, and resources.
- They are diligent and disciplined with how and where they spend their time.
- They do not allow unexpected obstacles to slow them down. When faced with roadblocks, distractions, and surprises, they improvise, adapt, overcome, and do what it takes to achieve mission objective.
- They do not blame others.
- They do not make excuses.

With a command mind-set, you'll fiercely protect the Golden Hours. You'll say "no" a lot. When a fellow recruiter stops by to chat you up about the weekend or gripe about how "no one can pass the test," you will no longer engage. When leaders attempt to dump busy work on you, you'll have the courage and confidence to push back respectfully.

You'll embrace a Daily Battle Rhythm that allows you to squeeze as much out of the Golden Hours as possible by managing the limited time that you have for recruiting wisely.

You will make mission, fast.

PART V

Targeting

10 | Targeting—Leveraging the Prospecting Pyramid

The only difference between a mob and a trained army is organization.
—Calvin Coolidge

"If you don't know where you're going, you might end up someplace else." The great Yankees catcher Yogi Berra said those words. Sadly, this is how many recruiters approach prospecting—hoping, praying, and spraying. No plan, no direction, and no strategy.

For far too many recruiters, there is no rhyme or reason to their prospecting pattern. No plan. No objective. Just going through the motions. The result is a miserable prospecting experience, a weak pipeline, and desperation interviews with poorly qualified prospects—just to get any sort of win.

Here are a few questions to consider:

- When you get into the office in the morning and organize your prospecting block, which prospects do you decide to contact first?
- When you hit the phones, schools, and streets, how do you know who you want to talk to and why?
- What's your strategy for building effective prospecting lists?

The bottom line is, if you don't have a plan and you don't know your objectives, your prospecting blocks will be far less effective.

When you build more effective prospecting lists, with clear objectives centered on specific prospecting channels, your prospecting blocks are easier, faster, more impactful, and generate far better results.

A simple rule of thumb to remember is: *Better list, better outcome.*

When I'm training recruiters to strategically target prospects, I begin by drawing a triangle (pyramid) on a whiteboard. Then I ask, "When you pick up the phone to make a prospecting attempt, how do you decide which prospect to call first?"

Invariably I'm met with blank stares.

"Okay, let me ask this a different way. Ideally, if you could call any list of prospects, which ones would you want on your list?"

This question gets them thinking a little harder. Someone will usually blurt out, "The ones most likely to enlist and ship immediately?"

"Bingo! That is exactly right." I respond.

Then I asked my next question: "How might you identify the prospects who have the highest probability of enlisting?"

From the back of the room, and evoking laughter, "The ones that can get past MEPS."

Someone else, "Prospects who have high test scores."

"Prospects with prior service."

"Prospects who come from referrals."

"Leads we need to follow up on from last week's community event."

"Grads who've just completed their first semester in college."

"Prospects who are fully qualified, but we've been unable to set an interview with them."

Now they're thinking.

Walk Like an Egyptian: Managing the Prospecting Pyramid

Recruiters who struggle with prospecting view their prospect database as a square. In other words, they treat every prospect exactly the same. For this reason, they attack their territory and prospect database randomly—with no system and no objective.

There are several problems with this approach. First, it is statistically inefficient. When prospecting activity is random, you might call a prospect who is ready to move forward, or you might not. However, because only a small number of your prospects will be qualified *and* in the window of opportunity at any given time, the statistical probability that you will call poorly qualified prospects is high. The result is ineffective prospecting blocks that make you feel like you are getting nowhere, far more rejection, and low productivity. Your recruiting results, confidence, and self-esteem all suffer.

Ultra-high performers have no interest in hunting and pecking for opportunities, so they design their lists to make prospecting blocks efficient and effective. They segment their prospects by:

- Lead source
- Potential to ship immediately
- Qualification
- Geography
- Situation
- Phase Line

- Window of enlistment opportunity (WEO)—the time period when the probability that the prospect will enlist is highest.
- Annual recruiting cycle (ARC) based on the school year.

They organize their prospecting block to get themselves in position to win by focusing on and building a pipeline of qualified prospects who have the highest probability of enlisting and shipping. Fanatical military recruiters view their prospect database as a pyramid.

- At the *bottom* of the pyramid are the thousands of prospects they know little about other than name and perhaps some contact information. They don't even know if the information about the prospect is correct (and there is a good chance that it isn't) and have little qualifying information.
  - *Action:* The goal with these prospects is to move them up the pyramid by gathering information so the recruiter can correct and confirm data, fill in the missing pieces, and begin the qualifying process.
- *Higher up* the pyramid, the information improves. There is solid contact information, including phone numbers, social media profiles, and e-mail addresses. There may be information on test scores, height and weight, parents, etc.
  - *Action:* The goal with these prospects is to identify the window of opportunity to enlist (WEO), motivations, fit, and additional qualifying information.
- Moving *even higher up*, most qualifying information has been identified. There are complete contact records, including social profiles. You've more than likely spoken to these prospects in the past at events, at school, or by phone.
  - *Action:* Your focus at this level is to implement nurturing campaigns to stay in front of these prospects in anticipation of a future WEO.
- *Further up* are Alphas. This is a highly targeted list of the identified Alphas, including fully qualified grads and prior service

prospects in your territory. There will be a limited number of these highly qualified prospects.

- *Action*: The focus for these prospects includes nurturing and regular touches, monitoring for trigger events, and building familiarity. You will be actively pursuing these prospects based on where you are in the annual recruiting cycle (ARC).

■ *Closer to the top* are HOT inbound leads and referrals.

- *Action*: These prospects require immediate follow-up to qualify and/or move them into the funnel.

■ *At the tip-top* of the prospecting pyramid are highly qualified prospects who are moving into the WEO due to impending graduation, financial issues (grads), or trigger events (life changes for grads and prior service), or hot leads who have self-identified a readiness to enlist now.

- *Action*: These are your highest priority prospects and should be on the top of your daily prospecting list. The goal is to get them in to conduct an interview.

The key to leveraging the prospecting pyramid method is a systematic daily focus on gathering qualifying information that identifies WEO and moves prospects up the pyramid based on this information over the course of the ARC.

Powerful Lists Get Powerful Results

Far too often, recruiters are prospecting from poorly constructed lists or, in many cases, no list at all. Building effective and robust prospecting lists requires consistent effort and discipline, which is why recruiters don't do it. It's so much easier to be random.

Heed this wake-up call. When you build powerful lists, you get powerful results. The quality of the list you work from during each prospecting block has a more significant impact on prospecting success than any other element except your mind-set.

Being a more efficient and effective prospector begins and ends with an organized, targeted prospecting list. A high-quality prospecting list is like a track for your prospecting train. It eliminates wasted time hunting and pecking for qualified prospects and helps you focus on a specific objective within a particular prospecting channel.

Lists can be constructed based on the following filters (or other methodologies to match to your unique situation). Use these elements in combination to structure your prospecting lists for maximum impact.

- Prospecting objective: Set an interview, qualify, build familiarity, nurture
- Prospecting channel: Phone, e-mail, social, text, face-to-face
- Qualification level: Highest qualified at the top of the list (Alphas and Unicorns)—least qualified at the bottom of the list (Bravos and Cat-4s)
- WEO: Highest probability to enlist in the immediate future at the top of the list—lowest probability at the bottom of the list
- Territory plan: Day of week, postal code, street, geographic grid, city
- Annual recruiting cycle
- School
- Category (high school, grad, prior service)
- Hot Leads (inbound)
- Referrals
- Event leads
- Mission directive

Some of these filters can be automated in your branch's RISS, while others may require manual decisions. Automate the process as much as possible with preset filters, views, and reports to make it easy to pull lists based on your prospecting objectives.

Only a handful of prospects in your database at any given time are in the window for immediate enlistment, and you've got to get in front of them before the window closes or they choose another career path or branch. Start each prospecting block focused on a list of these top-of-pyramid prospects while you are fresh, motivated, and feeling your best.

Because these prospects are inside the WEO, you will find it much easier to convert them into an interview. Starting your prospecting blocks by calling the prospects on the top of your pyramid will deliver early wins. These wins give you confidence and motivation to keep prospecting.

Once you have exhausted your high-potential prospects, shift your focus to prospects you are nurturing for the future. Follow that by focusing on qualifying the prospects lower on the pyramid.

Each day, if you begin at the top of the pyramid and set quality interviews, you will have time left over to systematically qualify the other prospects in your database, eventually moving them to the top of your pyramid. Over time, you'll experience more successful prospecting blocks, a dynamic prospect database, and a full pipeline.

Tomorrow, when you get ready to make your prospecting calls, take a look at the first name on your list and ask yourself, "Is this the best prospect to call?" Then get familiar with the filters and sort tools on your branch's RISS and build your own prospecting pyramid.

The Recruiting Information Support System Is Your Most Valuable Recruiting Tool

Each branch of the US Armed Forces uses its own Recruiting Information Support System (RISS):

> **ARISS**—Army and National Guard Recruiting Information Support System. (This acronym is still commonly used, but it's not as common as just calling it "The Box.")
>
> **AFRISS**—Air Force Recruiting Information Support System.

MCRISS—Marine Corps Recruiting Information Support System.

RTOOLS—Recruiting Tools (Navy).

For the sake of clarity, I use the acronym RISS (Recruiting Information Support System) to refer collectively to all of these recruiting databases. Compared to similar systems in the commercial world, the military has given you a nuclear arsenal, while civilians are operating with bows and arrows.

There is no weapon or tool in your recruiting arsenal that is more important or has more impact on your ability to consistently make mission than your RISS. Nothing. Your database of prospects is what helps you make mission now and in the future. No matter which branch you are in, a well-managed, living, breathing prospect database is a gold mine that keeps on giving.

Your RISS:

- Identifies high-value prospects.
- Helps you systematically qualify prospects so that you can move them up the prospecting pyramid.
- Allows you to segment and sort your prospect database and build prospecting lists based on any field or group of fields in the database. These targeted lists make you exponentially more effective and efficient in your prospecting activities.
- Allows you to manage the details and tasks related to many different contacts without having to remember everything.
- Keeps you organized and manages your long-term prospect pipeline and immediate applicant funnel.
- Helps you nurture and maintain relationships with schools and your community.
- Helps you manage your activity along the ARC.
- Makes life easier by doing work for you.

When you peel all of the technology away, the RISS is just a software-based filing system that makes it easier for you to manage and access information because it does a very simple task: It remembers important things for you and reminds you *when* those things are important.

Face it; you are moving fast and forget things. In recruiting, the little things are big things, and a well-managed RISS will prevent slip-ups that could cost you enlistments.

A Trash Can or a Gold Mine

More often than not, though, recruiters treat the RISS like a trash can rather than a gold mine. Call notes aren't entered. Records aren't kept up to date. Calls are not logged. This inattention to detail undermines the value and integrity of the database, leaving you struggling to engage the right prospects, at the right time, with the right message. It inhibits your ability to penetrate your schools effectively and develop advocates within them.

Gathering information and qualifying are where managing and building your database really pay off. Over time, through relentless prospecting and research, you'll gain a clear picture that helps you fully qualify the prospects in your schools and territory.

Building a database is like filling in a jigsaw puzzle. It takes time and lots of work, and sometimes there is not much evidence that it is paying off. The key here is faith and recognizing the cumulative impact of small wins, a little bit every day.

When it comes to building a powerful prospect database, my philosophy is simple: Put every detail about every prospect, every educator, every school administrator, every community partner, and every interaction into your RISS. Make good, clear notes. Never procrastinate. Do not take shortcuts. Develop the discipline to do it right the first time, and it will pay off for you over time.

Own It!

Here's the truth about the RISS: If you don't *own* it, you will never reach your true potential as a recruiter. Owning it means applying the command mind-set we discussed earlier. It means:

- Being accountable for maintaining the integrity of your prospect and school database.
- Not waiting until your NCOIC is screaming at you because you haven't updated a record in a month.
- Taking time to make copious notes during recruiting calls and logging those calls.
- Being meticulous about updating and adding information on educators, administrators, and community partners.
- Putting new leads in the system rather than carting around a pocket full of sticky notes with information you've collected from prospects.
- Rather than sitting around whining about how you don't understand the RISS, taking the time to dive in and learn how to use it.

Fanatical military recruiters own their database and lists. They own them because they get it. Their database is where targeted lists come from. The RISS makes them more efficient and effective. It should be so important to you that you eat, sleep, and drink it.

Some recruiters don't see how the system benefits them personally. They've always got someone on their case about updating the RISS, but in their minds they're doing it for the bureaucracy—not themselves. It's a mind-set issue. These recruiters see themselves "working for the man," whereas fanatical military recruiters believe that they are the commander of their territory.

I can get on my soapbox and preach. I can warn you of the consequences. I can explain the benefits. But the only person who can motivate you to exploit your RISS fully and invest diligently in building a quality database is you. If you choose not to invest in your RISS, as the saying goes, you can't fix stupid.

11

Yes Has a Number

You don't have to swing hard to hit a home run. If you got the timing, it'll go.
—Yogi Berra, baseball great

If we were to walk down a crowded street in New York City during rush hour and ask people to sing "Mary Had a Little Lamb" while we captured it on video, we'd get a lot of *no*s (see Figure 11.1) and more than a few *FU*s along the way.

Someone, though, would eventually say *yes*. It's just basic statistics. If you ask enough people, someone will do it. In recruiting, the more people you talk to, the more people you will enlist. That's how statistics work. It's just math. No matter what you are asking for, if you ask enough times, eventually you'll get a *yes*.

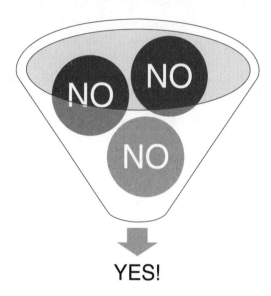

Figure 11.1   It takes many *nos* to get to a *yes*.

Yes has a number. The "Mary-Had-a-Little-Lamb" number, by the way, is eleven. On average, over several experiments, it took eleven requests to get one person to sing for me.

Keeping it real, though, the same can be said of playing the lottery. The statistics reveal that if you play enough times or scratch enough tickets, you will eventually win. It's just a stupid way to get rich, which is why, statistically speaking, rich people don't play the lottery. Instead, they invest their money where the odds are more in their favor.

Understanding probability is how ultra-high performing military recruiters play the game of recruiting. They work relentlessly to bend the *yes* number in their favor. In recruiting, the formula for making mission fast is simple:

> *Reduce* the chance of getting a *no*, while *increasing* the probability of getting a *yes*, *without decreasing* the number of times you ask.

This formula is the real secret to accelerating performance and crushing mission. But, and this is very important, you will never reach this level of optimization until you know your numbers.

Recruiting Is Governed by Numbers

Take a moment and think of your favorite professional athletes. If we were to ask them to tell us about their latest stats, what's the probability that they'd be able to recite a litany of detailed statistics on their performance?

I'll guarantee it would be 100 percent. Elite athletes know their numbers because their entire focus as competitors is on reaching peak performance. Knowing their numbers gives them the data they need to evaluate how they are doing at any given time and, most importantly, where to make adjustments to improve outcomes and performance.

It is no different in recruiting. Whereas connecting emotionally with other human beings, influencing them, and helping them make positive career choices is the art of recruiting, numbers are the science.

Elite recruiters, like elite athletes, track everything—as do elite recruiting teams. You will never reach peak performance until you know your numbers *and* leverage that data to analyze performance and make directional corrections.

Your *yes* number must be tracked all the way through the conversion funnel:

- Outbound prospecting attempts (by channel)
- Contacts
- Interviews set
- Interviews conducted
- Packets created
- Applicants to MEPS

- Enlistments
- Shipped

Let's be clear. This isn't anything you don't already know. If you've been in military recruiting for more than five minutes, you know that numbers matter. You know that it is stupid not to know your numbers. You know that ultra-high-performing recruiters, like elite athletes, are obsessed with numbers.

Yet despite a nearly universal understanding of conversion funnels and ratios among recruiters, many recruiters don't consistently track their numbers and use that information to make adjustments. If this is you, then you are abdicating your responsibility to your team, yourself, and your country.

You should be able to look down at your desk, on a simple piece of paper, and know exactly where you stand at any given moment, so *you* can quickly adjust to improve performance.

But it's easier not to keep track, because delusion is more comfortable than the cold edge of reality. But as you've already learned, in recruiting, you cannot be delusional and successful at the same time.

Develop the courage to face the truth—even when the truth tells you that you are not performing at your best. Be honest with yourself about where you really stand against your targets and what you need to do or sacrifice to get back on track if you are missing mission.

Yes has a number, but that number is not static. *You can change it.* But you cannot change what you cannot see. This is why you *must* know exactly what your *yes* number is at each step of the recruiting funnel. This awareness changes everything.

It's All About the Ratios

When you first dive into your numbers, there is also the human tendency to overanalyze, make too many assumptions (especially when the data isn't giving you a pretty story), or get caught up in the human

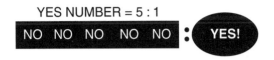

Figure 11.2   An example of the ratio of *nos* to *yeses*.

confirmation bias and arrange the data to tell the story that matches your rose-colored (and delusional) view of the situation.

When it comes to recruiting numbers, your confirmation bias is especially dangerous and the enemy of the truth. You'll tell yourself that "the reason my recruiting results are so bad is that I can't find anyone to pass the test." Instead of the real truth: "I'm barely prospecting and when I am, I'm fishing in the wrong pond."

The key to awareness is letting go of your ego and getting real about where you really stand and the activities that are leading to mission failure.

A ratio measures how much of one thing there is compared to another thing.[1] For example, for every five *nos* you hear, you get one *yes* (see Figure 11.2).

The *mission acceleration* process begins with analyzing your ratios top to bottom, across the entire recruiting funnel or MAP (Mission Accomplish Plan). Then shifting from the big-picture conversion funnel and looking more closely at your micro-ratios. This helps you focus on the nuances of performance. At the micro level, you make small tweaks in your activity or techniques that, in aggregate, deliver massive performance improvements—often doubling or tripling productivity.

It all begins with gaining a clear picture of the ratios in your unique conversion formula. For example:

- Prospecting attempts **to** contacts
- Contacts **to** interviews set
- Interviews set **to** conducts
- Lead sources **to** test passes

- Conducts **to** packets
- Packets **to** MEPS
- MEPS **to** enlistments
- Enlistments **to** shipped

Once you are tracking your numbers consistently, the door is opened to an honest assessment of both the efficiency and the effectiveness of your recruiting activities.

> *Efficiency* is how many attempts you are making to get a *yes*.
>
> *Effectiveness* is the ratio between the amount of activity and the number of *yeses (positive outcomes)* you get.

As you gain a deeper understanding of the ratio of total attempts to *yeses* and successful outcomes at each level of your conversion funnel, you may then begin addressing the variables that impact performance.

The key is pulling the right levers, at the right time, to improve the right ratios that have the greatest impact on performance, while minimizing negative consequences to other ratios.

For example: Perhaps you see an opportunity to improve the *contact-to-interview ratio* at the top of the conversion funnel, but you'll need to pull this lever without compromising the *call-to-contact ratio*. Otherwise the improved contact-to-interview ratio may be offset by a precipitous decrease in call volume that cancels out the entire effort.

This exercise of gaining a clear and honest picture of your ratios is crucial to wiping away the fog of delusion and false positives.

Changing Your *Yes* Number

To change your *yes* number, you must focus on optimizing the ratio between the two Es—efficiency and effectiveness. You must continue adjusting until the balance between the number of *yes* attempts and the number of positive outcomes maximizes your recruiting efforts and allows you to consistently make mission.

Once you know your numbers, you gain the power to consider objectively the variables that impact productivity. With this information, you'll make small adjustments that bend the probability of a win in your favor and increase or even double your *yes* number.

12 | Qualifying: Talking to the Right People

Victorious warriors win first and then go to war, while defeated warriors go to war first and then seek to win.

—Sun Tzu, Chinese military strategist

Recruiting is a blend of art and science. The art is influencing people to make commitments. The science is finding the right people to influence.

It's true that the more people you talk to, the more people you will enlist. That will not change. But I need to make something very clear. Nothing you learn in this book matters a hill of beans if you are not dealing with qualified prospects.

You can be the greatest prospector the world has ever known, but if you are dealing with a prospect who is not going to get past MEPS or who is unmotivated, and unwilling to engage, make micro-commitments, and advance through the process, you are going to fail. Period, end of story.

I know that you know this because it was beaten into you the moment you went to recruiting school to learn how to be a recruiter.

Ultra-high performers understand that *time is mission* and it is a waste of time to work with prospects who are unmotivated and not going to enlist. They know that qualified prospects are scarce, and investing too much time with a low-probability prospect takes them away from their most important task—prospecting to identify qualified prospects who can and will enlist.

But effective qualifying requires far more than just a quick profile, blueprint, or APPLEMDT on the phone. That's only part of it. It begins with gathering information while prospecting. It continues during your initial interview and requires maintaining acute awareness throughout the entire recruiting process for signs that might disqualify your applicant or lower the probability of a win.

Don't Swing at Nothing Ugly

I'm a big fan of Little League baseball. It is a rite of passage that helps kids build character, hone their values, and learn how to win and lose.

Several years back, when my son played Little League, we were fortunate to be on a team with great coaches who invested their time to help our sons learn to love the game. Along the way, they helped our tight-knit group of parents learn a few lessons, too.

In one of our most intense games, we were in the bottom of the final inning with two outs and the bases loaded. The game was tied. With the winning run on third base, all we needed was a hit to win the game and advance to the playoffs.

As our next batter walked from the dugout toward the batter's box, Coach Sandro pulled him aside for one last pep talk. He kneeled in front of the ten-year-old young man, grabbed a handful of his jersey near the collar, and gave him some sage advice.

"Whatever you do," Coach Sandro admonished, "don't swing at nothing ugly."

It was profound advice for batters and recruiters.

If you've ever played baseball or softball or watched your kids play, you've no doubt witnessed a player chasing a wild pitch—too high, too low, or way outside of the strike zone. The awkward swing of the bat, swishing through thin air, leaves the player off balance and embarrassed. It is sometimes funny to watch, but mostly the fans, coaches, and players emit a collective groan and wonder why in the world the player took a swing at that pitch.

It is no different in recruiting. Each day, recruiters waste time, energy, and emotion swinging at applicants who have little chance of making it past the floor. Sadly, the results are predictable. These recruiters strike out.

This is exactly why effective qualifying was a front-and-center lesson in recruiting school. It's easy for new recruiters to waste time on prospects who are not qualified.

We know that the more *qualified* people you talk to, the more people you will enlist. The problem is that far too many recruiters use qualifying as an excuse not to talk to people. Qualifying is a wall they put between themselves and human engagement. The result is they have far fewer face-to-face interviews than ultra-high performers.

Moneyball

"Two" blurted out Sergeant First Class Ramirez in response to my question, his right hand raised with two fingers up.

My question: "How many qualification questions do you need to ask on a prospecting call to make the decision to set up an interview?"

"I just need height and weight." He was shaking his head incredulously at the other recruiters in the room who argued that they had to complete an APPLEMDT questionnaire in its entirety before setting up an interview.

A Staff Sergeant in the back of the room shouted out, "Three." "Which three?" I asked.

"Height, weight, and have you been arrested. The schools where I recruit have a high instance of arrests." he responded.

When I poll recruiters on what they need to know about a prospect before conducting an interview, there are consistently two schools of thought:

1. They need to know just enough about the prospect to conduct an interview.
2. The prospect must be fully and completely qualified before conducting an interview.

In 2002, Billy Beane, the general manager for the Oakland A's, changed Major League Baseball forever with his sabermetric approach to scouting and building a winning baseball team with limited resources. His story was chronicled in the movie *Moneyball*, which was based on Michael Lewis's book *Moneyball: The Art of Winning an Unfair Game*.

Beane's analysis demonstrated that on-base percentage (OBP) was the best indicator of success when evaluating a player's ability to contribute and be productive. It was a radical departure from the traditional model and stats used for scouting. Two years later, in 2004, the Boston Red Sox adopted Beane's approach on their way to winning the World Series and breaking the Curse of the Bambino.

The OBP of military recruiting is the interview. The recruiters with the highest percentage of interview conducts are, almost always, the highest-performing recruiters—the ultra-high performers. The interview is, essentially, getting on base. It's simple and intuitive. The more times you get on base, the more opportunities you have to score.

Clearly you should not waste time with applicants who cannot or will not enlist. The most expensive waste of time in recruiting is to spend it with the wrong prospect. But poor-performing recruiters take this to the extreme. They allow qualification to become a reason not to talk to people.

Poor performers usually have a low number of attempts to begin with—a bad thing. But when low activity is combined with a low *contact to conduct* ratio, it becomes almost impossible to make mission.

The Balance and Nuance of Qualifying

Qualifying prospects is about balance. You want to get enough information to avoid interviewing candidates who are completely unqualified but not allow hard qualifying questions to chase good prospects away or put them in a position where they lie to you.

You want to schedule as many face-to-face interviews as possible. This means some prospects will be disqualified during the initial interview or during subsequent steps of the recruiting process. *This does not mean that you should throw mud at the wall by sending every applicant who can fog a mirror to MEPS.*

Ultra-high performers know *three things* about interviews:

1. The recruiting process begins with the interview. This is why a recruiter who conducts many face-to-face interviews will beat out the recruiter who conducts only a few interviews because "no one is qualified," every time.
2. When faced with tough qualifying questions, prospects will tell you one thing on the phone and something completely different in person. You'll get far better information during a face-to-face interview than in a quick prospecting conversation.
3. When you conduct an interview, if the prospect is unqualified to move forward, you may, at a minimum, be able to flip the interview into a referral.

There is not a one-size-fits-all solution for qualifying in every recruiting situation. Every market is different.

In recruiting, context matters. Each prospect, conversation, zip code, territory, school, or recruiting segment is different and requires recruiters to adapt and adjust to those unique situations. If you work in the inner city, past run-ins with law enforcement may be more prevalent than if you are working in a rural area. In the suburbs, ADHD drug usage may occur at higher rates than in the inner city. Height and weight may be a much bigger issue in some zip codes than others.

Depending on your branch, battalion, or company, your leaders may have different requirements for qualifying. And mission? That's always a moving target.

I'm certainly not going to tell you how to initially qualify before setting up an interview. You need to determine what works best based on your unique situation.

It's about developing a qualification routine that gives you the highest probability of setting an interview with a qualified prospect while using the lowest number of hard qualification questions during the initial prospecting engagement.

If every prospect must be 100 percent qualified before any interview, it's unlikely that you'll be speaking to very many people. Because you'll:

- Turn off people who don't want a proctology exam before they meet to learn more about a career in the military.
- Disqualify people who may eligible once you get more information.
- Miss opportunities for getting referrals from prospects.
- Get burned because people will hide crucial information from you.

It's also important to remember that effective qualification is not a single decision point at a single place in time; rather it's an ongoing series of decisions along the entire recruiting journey.

Your branch's qualifying format or process may help you decide if the prospect qualifies to join your branch of the military on paper, but it doesn't tell you if your prospect is engaged, willing, and motivated to join the military. That happens during your interviews and as you build a relationship with your prospects.

Never forget that prospects enlist first with *you* and then the military.

13 | Prospecting Balance and Objectives

We're living at a time when attention is the new currency. Those who insert themselves into as many channels as possible, look set to capture the most value.
—Pete Cashmore, founder of mashable.com

When it comes to prospecting, there is one overriding objective: Be as efficient and effective as possible. In other words, do as much prospecting activity as possible, in the least amount of time possible, while generating the best outcomes possible.

Efficiency is a product of time discipline. It requires blocking your time, eliminating distractions, planning in advance, and concentrating your focus.

Effectiveness increases with:

- Targeting
- Better lists

- Balancing prospecting across multiple channels (telephone, face-to-face, text, e-mail, social)
- The quality of your prospecting skills
- How effectively you leverage prospecting frameworks
- Your ability to manage your disruptive emotions
- Honing your message
- Gaining clarity on the prospecting objective

Knowing your objective for each call makes you more efficient because you are able to build prospecting blocks and group your prospecting activity around those objectives. This allows you to move faster and make more prospecting touches in less time.

Developing a defined objective makes you effective because on each prospecting phone call, face-to-face approach, text message, e-mail, social media touch, event, or referral request, you know exactly what to ask for and how to give your prospect a compelling reason to accept your request.

The *objective* is the primary outcome you expect from your prospecting touch. There are three core prospecting objectives:

1. Set an appointment for an interview
2. Gather qualifying information
3. Build familiarity

Set an Appointment

The most valuable activity in the recruiting process is setting an appointment for an interview. The one commonality among ultra-high-performing recruiters is that they conduct far more interviews than average recruiters.

Gather Information and Qualify

Prospecting conversations are the most effective way to gather information about potential recruits and filter out prospects who have no chance of joining your branch of the service. But be careful: Mediocre recruiters default to qualifying, while ultra-high performing recruiters default to conducting the interview.

Build Familiarity

Familiarity plays an important role in getting prospects to engage. Familiarity breeds liking. The more familiar a prospect is with you, your branch, and military career opportunities in general, the more likely they will be willing to accept and return your calls, reply to your e-mails, accept a social media connection request, respond to a text message, and engage when you are at events and prospecting in person.

Building familiarity is a secondary objective of a prospecting touch. Familiarity as a prospecting objective requires a long-term focus, because it is developed through the cumulative impact of ongoing prospecting activity. This is why savvy recruiting professionals cross-leverage prospecting channels to systematically build familiarity.

- Each time your phone number pops up on your prospect's phone screen, it creates familiarity.
- Each time you leave a voice mail and they hear your voice and name, familiarity increases.
- Each time you send an e-mail or message, they read your name and see your e-mail address and service branch, and their familiarity with you increases.

- When you connect with them on Facebook, Instagram, or other social media sites, familiarity increases.
- When you like, comment on, or share something they post on a social media channel, familiarity increases.
- When you meet them at a school event or career fair and put a face with a name, familiarity increases.
- Your community and school marketing efforts increase familiarity.

Prospecting Is Not Pitching

Prospecting is not an opportunity for a kitchen-sink data dump of everything about you and your branch. It is not the time when you pitch, tell your story, or spend an hour chatting it up with a prospect. That's what face-to-face interviews are for. Instead, your primary objective is to get an appointment for an interview.

Prospecting shuns the nuance, art, and finesse of moving a prospect through the recruiting funnel from prospect, to applicant, to the floor, to shipped. To be effective, you've got to know what you want and ask for it. To be efficient, you must get in as many prospecting touches as possible during each prospecting block.

Prospecting is for rapid qualifying and asking for time. You don't need brilliant scripts. You don't need complex strategies. You don't need to overcomplicate it. You've got to get to the point, ask for what you want, and move on to the next touch.

Adopt a Balanced Prospecting Methodology

"But Jeb, I'm so much better in person!"
"But Jeb, Facebook works better than the phone."
"But Jeb, I do most of my prospecting via text."

But Jeb, but Jeb, but Jeb. I've heard the same refrain from hundreds of recruiters who are quick to tell me that they are so much better at one type of prospecting or another.

The "I'm so much better at . . ." excuse is just that: an excuse to avoid the other prospecting techniques that those recruiters find unpalatable. More often than not, it's an excuse to avoid phone prospecting.

The size of the funnel always reveals the truth. Recruiters who gravitate to a single prospecting methodology deliver suboptimal performance.

I can guarantee that when the words "But you don't understand, I'm so much better at . . ." come out of a recruiter's mouth in response to a prospecting technique I've just introduced, that recruiter is underperforming against mission.

So instead of making excuses about how you are so much better at one type of prospecting or another, you should be actively focused on balancing prospecting across the various prospecting channels to give yourself the highest probability of engaging the highest qualified prospects in the crowded, hyper-competitive marketplace.

The Fallacy of Putting All Your Eggs in One Basket

Imagine that a friend comes to you seeking advice on investing for retirement. They explain that they went to a financial seminar where an investment "guru" presented a "sure-thing stock." The guru advised everyone to immediately move their entire nest egg into this stock. What would you say?

If you were a good friend, you would be incredulous. "Putting your money into a single stock is stupid. You'll lose your retirement money!" you'd admonish.

"But the guru says this investment is a sure thing," your friend responds emphatically. "He says I can make a ton of money!"

You grab him by the collar and shake him. "Are you kidding me? Are you a moron? There are no sure things in investing. That's why sane people diversify—they spread their money out across multiple investments to reduce risk. This guy is feeding you a line of bull. If you follow his advice, you're courting financial disaster."

In recruiting, consistently relying on a single prospecting methodology (usually the one you feel generates the least amount of resistance and rejection), at the expense of others, consistently generates mediocre results. However, balancing your prospecting regimen across multiple channels gives you a statistical advantage that almost always leads to higher performance over the long term.

Avoid the Lunacy of One Size Fits All

The foundation of a winning prospecting strategy is balance. Think of me as your friend, grabbing you by the collar and shaking you into reality. Putting all your prospecting eggs into a single basket is stupid. It's mission suicide. Using the "I'm better at . . ." excuse to run from prospecting techniques you don't like is short-sighted.

Ultra-high performers have mastered balanced prospecting in the same manner that wealthy people have mastered balance in their investment portfolios. Balancing prospecting across multiple channels gives you the greatest statistical probability of engaging the right prospecting, at the right time, with the right message.

Your prospecting routine should include a mixture of:

- Telephone
- Face-to-face
- E-mail
- Social Media
- Text Messaging
- Referrals
- Networking
- Inbound "Hot" Leads

- Direct Mail
- School and Community Events

The relative distribution of your time investment in each prospecting methodology should be based on your unique situation.

There isn't a one-size-fits-all formula for balanced prospecting. Every territory, mission directive, and prospect base is different, as are the cycles of the school and calendar year. The demands of mission change over time, as will your prospecting routine. It's also important to have a clear understanding of where you are against mission target because that may also determine the appropriate mix of prospecting channels.

The key is designing your prospecting regimen based on what works best in your market or geographic area. Likewise, tenure in your territory matters. If you are new to recruiting, or have just taken over a new territory, your balance of prospecting techniques will likely be different than that of a tenured recruiter who has been working the same territory for a year or two.

Striking a balanced approach with prospecting, however, is the most effective means of filling your recruiting funnel. With few exceptions, the combination of multiple techniques and channels is the most effective path to reaching qualified prospects and consistently making mission.

PART VI

Pick Up the Phone!

14

Telephone Prospecting Excellence

If the phone doesn't ring it's me.

—Jimmy Buffett

Question: "What's the easiest way to get a recruiter to stop working?"

Answer: "Put a phone in front of them."

This joke is all too true for thousands of recruiters for whom picking up the phone and calling a prospect is the most stressful part of their day. These reluctant recruiters procrastinate—get ducks in a row, work to ensure that everything is perfect before they dial, default to social media, and secretly hope that the phone will disappear.

They make excuses—and I mean *any* excuse—to do anything other than call prospects.

They work over their leaders, too. Whining that no one answers the phone anymore. Arguing that calling is a waste of time. Complaining that people don't like to be contacted by phone.

Last month at a Fanatical Military Recruiting Boot Camp, a First Sergeant grabbed me before the session to thank me for being there. He then complained that the single biggest challenge facing the battalion was getting the recruiters to pick up the phone and call prospects.

His words: "We are having such a hard time getting them to just pick up the phone and talk to people. Most of them waste their days f#@king around on Facebook."

As soon as I began the module on telephone prospecting, the normal whining began about how teenagers don't answer the phone. Two recruiters (both egregiously behind on mission) insisted that social media was the only way to communicate with "this new generation."

I've heard it all before and I'm immune to excuses, because I know the truth. Nobody answers a phone that doesn't ring. Under-performing recruiters are always quick to complain that what they are *not* doing *isn't* working.

We did three live phone blocks that day using the targeted prospecting lists the recruiters had prepared in advance. Over the course of the day, we maintained a 41 percent contact rate—that's actual live prospects answering their phones—and a 47 percent appointment rate. This was *not* a statistical anomaly. It was generated by 82 recruiters who made 1,066 outbound dials (attempts).

Everyone was stunned at the results. The same First Sergeant pulled me aside before I left. "I don't understand how you got those results," he said. "Everybody tells me that people don't answer the phone anymore."

"Who's telling you that?" I asked.

"The recruiters," he responded.

"The same people that you say won't make calls?"

He nodded his head slowly as the weight of this realization sank in.

Nobody Answers a Phone That Doesn't Ring

The myth that the phone no longer works—because people don't answer—is disproven during our Fanatical Military Recruiting Boot Camps. Recently during an FMR training session in Georgia, we started phone blocks at 8 a.m. It was June, school was out, and we were calling high school students. When I gave the order—*you have 30 minutes to make 30 dials and set two interviews*—the hands went up and the grumbling began.

"Jeb, you know it's way too early to be calling."

"These kids are all still in bed."

"No one is going to answer the phone this early!"

"We shouldn't be calling this early because we'll be waking people up and upsetting them."

On and on it went until I cut it off and gave the order again: *Thirty minutes, thirty dials, two appointments. Go!*

Thirty minutes later, heads were shaking as the First Sergeants reported the numbers. As a group, in just 30 minutes, the recruiters had booked 73 interviews. Yes, we shook a few kids out of bed, but because most of them were sleeping with their phones, we had far more conversations than anyone anticipated. It turns out that no one in the battalion ever made prospecting calls that early in the morning.

The myth that the phone doesn't work is just that—a myth. The statistics don't lie. When working with military recruiters, we see between 20 and 50 percent contact rates by phone, depending on the quality of the list used while calling.

This is far higher than response rates with e-mail and social recruiting and provides a much faster path to qualifying the prospects and converting them to face-to-face interviews. Real-world evidence flies directly in the face of the myth, repeated over and over again, that the telephone has a low success rate with teenagers. If you analyze military recruiting data, you'll find that telephone prospecting generates more appointments than any other prospecting channel.

It gets even better. We are seeing clear trends that contact rates via phone are rising. More prospects are answering their phones because of three trends:

1. **Phones are anchored to people.** For your prospects, the smartphone is their closest companion. The average prospect looks at their phone every six minutes. They sleep with their phone, eat with their phone, and take it everywhere they go.
2. **No one is calling.** Because so much communication has shifted to e-mail, social in-boxes, and text, phones are not ringing. Because of this, recruiters who are calling are standing out in the crowd and getting through.
3. **Prospects are getting burned out on impersonal spam.** E-mail and social in-boxes are being flooded with crap. Prospects are hungry for something different—a live, authentic human being. They want to talk to *you*.

The Telephone Is, Has Always Been, and Will Continue to Be Your Most Powerful Recruiting Tool

Pay attention! The phone is your most powerful recruiting tool. Period, end of story.

Let me repeat this one more time, slowly, for the people in the back row who aren't tracking. There is no other tool in recruiting that will deliver better results, fill your funnel faster, and help you cover more ground in less time than the phone.

So, stop looking at it like it's your enemy! And no, it is not going to dial itself.

Here is the brutal truth: Recruiters who ignore the phone deliver mediocre results, consistently miss mission, and become a weak link.

Sergeant Gilroy wrote me with this question:

"My Gunnery Sergeant is always trying to get me to use the phone for prospecting. I'm terrible on the phone, and I've tried to explain to him that I'm much better in person. How can I convince him to just let me get out and talk to people face to face?"

This question is not unusual. When faced with telephone prospecting, many recruiters say, "But I'm way better in person."

My answer: Of course you are better in person. That is why you need to get out in the community, own your schools, and default to setting face-to-face interviews with qualified prospects and their parents.

But here's the deal: In recruiting, time is mission, and you can cover far more ground, qualify more prospects, and set more interviews in a focused and targeted one-hour phone block than in an entire day of driving around in your territory looking for face-to-face interactions.

Think about it this way: How many prospects could you reasonably engage and qualify prospecting face to face in an eight-hour period? Even on your busiest day, 20 would be a stretch. In most territories, with travel time, getting into your schools, and catching students in between classes, it would be closer to 10.

How about one hour on the phone, with a list of targeted prospects? How many phone calls could you make? Averaging one to two minutes per call, you could make 25 to 50 calls. So, if you are touching twice as many prospects in about a tenth of the time, in a climate-controlled environment, which do you think will yield better results? The answer is a no-brainer.

Am I saying that face-to-face prospecting, social recruiting, e-mail, or text messaging are bad prospecting channels and should not be used? Of course not. As you've already learned, when you balance your prospecting across multiple channels, you give yourself the highest statistical probability of reaching the right prospect, with the right message, at the right time.

What I am saying is that the phone is the most efficient prospecting tool because when you are organized, you can use it to reach more prospects in a shorter period of time than through any other prospecting channel. Because you have many more things to do in your recruiting day than prospect, it is in your best interest to use the most efficient method for contacting lots of prospects—and that's the phone.

The telephone is also more effective than e-mail, social, and text because actually speaking to another human being gives you a higher probability to make a personal connection and get the prospect in for an interview. Yet many recruiters find it awkward to use the phone for prospecting because they:

- Don't know what to say, say stupid things, or use awkward, cheesy scripts that generate resistance and rejection.
- Don't have an easy-to-execute telephone prospecting framework that actually works.
- Don't know how to deal with reflex responses, brush-offs, and objections.
- Find it uncomfortable and awkward to interrupt invisible strangers.
- Are afraid of rejection.

Nobody Likes It; Get Over It

Staff Sergeant Richmond hit me up with this question:

"Jeb, I need your advice. I know that I should be using the phone more for prospecting. But it's really difficult for me to make the call. I feel like that kid calling a girl to go to a school dance who gets rattled when her dad answers the phone and forgets what to say. I know it's all in my head. I'm normally very confident and comfortable talking to people. But when I'm on the phone with a prospect, it's a different story. How do I overcome this?"

Richmond's question is honest. It reflects how many recruiters feel about telephone prospecting.

Richmond, like most recruiters, has every intention of getting on the phone and engaging new prospects. But as he reluctantly dials that first number—after wasting prime recruiting time on "research" and "administrative" work in an effort to avoid the inevitable—his palms sweat, his heart pounds, and he secretly prays that no one will answer. Then the prospect or a parent says "Hello," and he freezes and forgets what to say. He stumbles over his words, stuttering and sputtering. The prospect quickly brushes him off:

> "I'm not interested."
> "I'm going to college."
> "I don't think the military is right for me."
> "I don't have time to talk."
> *Click.*

He feels rejected and embarrassed, and his motivation for calling evaporates. To avoid making more calls, he shuffles papers and wastes time doing anything but dialing again. He whines that he has no time to call because there is so much admin work to do, and instead of calling, he hangs out on Facebook.

I'm not going to sugarcoat it. Telephone prospecting is the most despised activity in recruiting. Calling and interrupting people you don't know is uncomfortable. You get a tremendous amount of rejection.

It will always be uncomfortable to pick up the phone and interrupt strangers. It is just not a natural thing to do. There will always be calls and even days when you fumble your words and become embarrassed. You will always get more rejection than acceptance. Nothing is going to change this. Yet the fact remains that the telephone is, by a wide margin, the most effective weapon in your recruiting arsenal.

What I find across the board, though, is that most recruiters don't know how to use the phone for prospecting. They've never been taught the frameworks required for efficient and effective outbound telephone prospecting.

My objective is to teach you telephone prospecting techniques that drive qualified applicants into your pipeline.

You'll start by learning how to leverage the telephone to maximize your recruiting day. I'm going to teach you how to double or even quadruple the number of dials you make in a much shorter period of time so that you can get your phone block knocked out and move on to other things that are far more enjoyable.

Then I'm going to teach you what to do and say when you get prospects on the phone. You will learn how to reduce resistance, increase the probability that you will achieve your defined objective, and mitigate rejection.

Finally, you will learn how to effectively deal with and get past reflex responses, brush-offs, and objections (RBOs) to more effectively set interviews and qualify.

Before moving forward, though, let's stipulate a few things:

- You are going to face a lot of rejection on the phone because, statistically speaking, you will generate more real-time interactions with prospects than through any other prospecting channel.
- Most of your calls will not get answered. You'll connect with between 20 percent and 50 percent of your prospects on average during phone blocks. This is why, when you get a prospect on the line, it counts.
- Most of the reason that you are frustrated with the phone and find making telephone prospecting calls abhorrent is because you or the people who taught you how to prospect are over-complicating the living stew out of a very simple, straightforward process.
- Nobody really likes telephone prospecting. No matter what I teach you, you will still dislike the phone. That doesn't negate

the fact that to reach peak recruiting performance, you must master telephone prospecting.

- If you want to make mission fast and deliver consistently, you've got to accept that telephone prospecting sucks and embrace it.

The Ultimate Key to Success Is the Scheduled Phone Block

Fanatical military recruiters set up daily phone blocks of one to two hours—usually one block first thing in the morning for grads and prior service and blocks in the afternoon and evening for students. During these set blocks, they remove all distractions—shutting off e-mail and mobile devices and letting those around them know that they are not to be disturbed. They set clear goals for how many dials they will make.

This call block is booked as a *set and unmovable* appointment on their calendar and it is sacred. Nothing interferes.

The most effective way to get the most out of call blocks is high-intensity prospecting sprints (HIPS). Break call blocks into small, manageable chunks, and set goals for those chunks. It is much easier to set a goal to make 15 telephone prospecting calls than 100. It's far more effective to make as many attempts in 15 or 30 minutes rather than slog through two straight hours.

It is much easier to overcome your initial fears and trepidations a few calls at time. You can wrap your mind around these small chunks.

Put your head down, remove distractions, and push hard during these HIPS; you'll make far more calls and set many more interviews than you thought possible.

Some people set an overall goal for each daily phone block. For example, they will decide in advance to make 50 dials. Next, they'll set smaller ten-dial blocks. Then they'll pump themselves up for these small blocks. When they finish, they give themselves a small reward and move to the next ten calls.

An easy way some recruiters manage their phone blocks is to count backwards from 50. You simply write the numbers 1–50 on a piece of paper. With each dial, you strike through its number, starting with 50 and work your way to one. Many people report that it is much easier to hit telephone prospecting goals using this technique.

No matter what technique you choose, though, schedule your phone blocks on the calendar. Make them appointments with yourself. Keep these appointments sacred and don't be late.

15

The Seven-Step Telephone Prospecting Framework

When you pick up the phone and call a prospect—cold, warm, hot, referral, follow-up, or inbound lead—and they are not expecting your call, you are an interruption.

Consider how you feel when your day is interrupted by someone calling you unannounced. It can make you feel irritated, angry, or resentful because, in most cases, the call comes when you are right in the middle of something else.

Let's step into your shoes. How do you want to be interrupted?

Okay, your first response is probably, "I wouldn't want to get the call in the first place." I'll give you that. No one wants to be interrupted—not me, not you, not your prospect—even if the call is something we welcome.

But let's get back to reality. Recruiters who don't interrupt prospects miss mission.

So, if you're going to get interrupted, what would you want? Think about it. You would want the caller to get right to the point and get off the phone quickly, so you could get back to posting cat videos on YouTube.

Now try standing in your prospect's shoes. They are people just like you who resent having their day interrupted by an unscheduled caller. Your focus, then, is to make the call quick and to the point, so that you achieve your objective and your prospect can get back to what they were doing.

Few things in recruiting have become more overcomplicated than the simple telephone prospecting call. Efficient and effective telephone prospecting should get you to yes, no, or maybe fast. It should allow you to qualify the prospect quickly, in the least intrusive way. You should be able to use a relaxed, confident, professional tone that reduces resistance and makes you sound like an authentic human being rather than a scripted robot.

To do this, you need a framework that is consistent and repeatable. A consistent, repeatable process takes pressure off you and your prospect. Because you are not winging it each time you call, you won't have to worry about what to say. And because you are focused and intentional, it is respectful of your prospect's time.

Shorter, more impactful calls mean you complete phone blocks faster, which in turn keeps your pipeline full and gives you more time to spend engaged in the activities that make recruiting fun. An effective telephone prospecting call might sound like this—a simple seven-step framework (see Figure 15.1):

1. **Get their attention by saying their name:** "Hi, Julie."
2. **Identify yourself:** "My name is Sergeant First Class Blount with the Georgia National Guard."
3. **Give the reason for your call:** "The reason I'm calling is to set up an interview with you."
4. **Bridge with a *because* statement:** "Because your test scores were excellent and may qualify you for a significant signing bonus."

Figure 15.1   Seven-Step Telephone Prospecting Framework

5. **Ask for the interview and shut up:** "How about we meet Wednesday afternoon around 3:00 p.m.?"
6. **Qualify:** "Before you come in, I have just a couple of questions for you. Is that okay?"
7. **Confirm or flip to a referral (if not qualified):** "Excellent, I'm looking forward to seeing you on Wednesday at 3:00 p.m. Please bring the following items with you."

Or if they are not qualified, flip to a referral.

"Thank you very much for taking time to speak with me. Based on what you are telling me about your medical history (or another disqualifier), it looks like you won't be eligible to join the military. I know that's disappointing. I'm sorry. I'm just curious, though; do you have any other friends who should be talking to me?

There is one point I want to be sure you get. There are no pauses between steps one through five. Do not stop until you ask for the interview. The moment you pause, you lose control of the call.

The prospect will throw out an objection or begin asking you questions. Your focus is getting a yes, no, or maybe on a commitment to meet with you—fast. Once you get the commitment, qualifying becomes easier, more transparent, and more truthful. As soon as your prospect answers the phone, you should walk through the first five steps of the framework without stopping.

Here is another example. In this case I'm calling an inbound lead:

> "Hi, Ian, this is Sergeant First Class Blount with the Georgia National Guard. The reason I'm calling is to grab a few minutes of your time for an interview because you expressed interest in learning more about joining the Guard. I've got an opening on my calendar on Thursday at 10 a.m. How about we get together then?"

If Ian agrees:

> "Excellent, Ian. Before you come in, I have a few questions I need to ask. Let's begin with your height and weight . . .?"

If Ian is qualified:

> "Ian, I'm really looking forward seeing you on Thursday at 10 a. m. Please bring the following items with you. . ."

Here is another example with a prior service prospect. My objective is to qualify and move them *directly into a recruiting conversation*:

> "Hi, Corrina, this is Sergeant First Class Blount from the Georgia National Guard. The reason I'm calling is to grab a few minutes of your time to learn more about you, because we're looking for people with prior military service and your qualifications. Tell me more about your current situation."

Telephone prospecting should be direct, professional, and straight to the point. There is no reason to overcomplicate it with cheeseball scripts that turn prospects off, create resistance, and make you look foolish.

Seven-Step Telephone Prospecting Framework

When you use the Seven-Step Telephone Prospecting Framework, you'll find that you stumble over your words less and achieve your objective more often.

A framework is like a set of rails that keeps you moving toward your objective. It makes you agile and adaptive because it can be leveraged across different situations—based on context—and frees you to focus on your message rather than the time-consuming effort of rethinking your process each time.

Let's take a closer look at the elements of the Seven-Step Telephone Prospecting Framework.

Get Their Attention

Once your prospect answers the phone, you have a split second to get their attention. The easiest, fastest way to get someone's attention is to use the most beautiful word in the world to them—their name.

Anywhere, anytime, when you say another person's name, they will sit up and look up. For that split second, you have their attention. The same dynamic is at play when telephone prospecting, and it is important to use this to your advantage. Just say: "Hi, Julie."

Important point: Notice that I didn't ask Julie, "How are you doing?"

There is a reason for this. When you interrupt a prospect's day, you get resistance. Resistance hits as soon as they realize that they made a big mistake by answering their phone. This realization comes to a crescendo right after you ask, "How are you today?" This creates an awkward and uncomfortable pause that usually results in you filling in the silence with pitching.

Your prospect was going about her morning happily when her phone rang, interrupting her day. As you asked, "How are you doing?" her get-away-from-this-interruption-fast mechanism kicks in. She hits you with a stern tone of voice, "Who is this?" setting you back on your heels and derailing the call.

That's how your prospect is doing and that's how you lose control of the call. Don't ask, "How are you doing?" and don't pause or leave any awkward silence. Say their name and keep moving.

Identify Yourself and Say Why You Are Calling

Get right to the point. Say your prospect's name, then tell her who you are and the reason you called. Transparency has two benefits:

1. It demonstrates that you are a professional and respect your prospect's time—save the idle chitchat for after you have established a real relationship.
2. By telling your prospect who you are and why you are calling, you reduce their stress, because people naturally abhor the unknown. They are more comfortable when they know what to expect.

The one thing that I know to be true is prospects are people just like you. They don't want to be tricked, they don't want to be manipulated, and they don't want to be interrupted. What they want is to be treated with respect. The best way you can show your respect is to be truthful, relevant, and to the point.

Bridge—Give Them a Because

Telephone prospecting should quickly engage a prospect and persuade them to give up their time. You don't need to craft elaborate pitches or come up with complicated scripts. In fact, this is where most prospecting goes wrong.

You are interrupting your prospect's day. Think about it. If a recruiter were interrupting your busy day, what would you want?

- You'd want them to be quick and get right to the point, so you could get back to your day.
- You'd want them to be clear and transparent about their intentions—to tell you exactly want they wanted.
- You'd want the interruption to be relevant to your situation, problems, or issues.

Your prospecting message must be quick, simple, direct, and relevant. The relevant part is the critical element. Prospects are going to agree to give up their valuable time for their reasons, not yours. The lower the risk to them for giving up their time, the more likely they'll be willing to meet with you.

You lower the risk for your prospect by answering the most important question on their mind—WIIFM: **W**hat's **in It for Me**?

Of course, it is not always possible to know which reason will lower the risk enough for your prospect to say yes to your request. You must invest time to define the possible reasons that would create enough WIIFM for them to give up their time to spend it with you.

WIIFM—*The Power of Because*

According to Robert Cialdini, author of *Influence*, "A well-known principle of human behavior says that when we ask someone to do us a favor, we will be more successful if we provide a reason. People simply like to have reasons for what they do."

In prospecting, all you've got to do is give your prospect a relevant reason to meet with you. It doesn't need to be perfect—just good enough to get the face-to-face interview.

I'm also realistic. To be efficient at prospecting, you've got to pack lots of prospecting touches into a short period of time. In most cases, you will be prospecting to a similar group of prospects who share a common set of issues. Stopping to craft a perfect, unique "because" statement for each one of these prospects is inefficient and impractical.

Instead, you need a set of simple yet compelling messages that work most of the time with most of your prospects depending on their situation—students, grads, prior service, Alphas, Unicorns, and inbound leads. The message has to be quick, direct, and persuasive, but it cannot sound like a cheesy script. It's got to be natural and authentic.

You need a message that can be delivered in 10 to 20 seconds and gives your prospect a reason or a "because" that's good enough to get them to say yes.

In a landmark study on human behavior, psychologist Ellen Langer and a team of researchers from Harvard demonstrated the raw power of because. Langer had her team of researchers cut in line in front of people waiting for access to photocopiers.

She discovered that when the researcher politely asked to jump in front of the person waiting for the copier without giving a reason—"Excuse me, I have five pages. May I use the copier?"—the person would say yes only about 60 percent of the time. However, when the researcher qualified the request with a valid reason— "because I'm in a hurry"—the person said yes, on average, 94 percent of the time.

Here's where the research became interesting. When the researcher gave a nonsensical reason like, "Excuse me, I have five pages. May I use the copier? *Because* I have to make copies," the person still said yes 93 percent of the time. It was a truly stunning finding. Saying the word *because*—giving a reason—was more important and powerful than the reason itself.

Now, I want to be absolutely clear that I am not advising you to make up nonsense and use that while prospecting. What I am saying is that delivering a simple, straightforward "because" statement works, and spending hours agonizing over some complex script is unlikely to give you anything more effective in prospecting than a simple, direct because.

For example, just saying, "I'd like to set up a short interview *because* I want to learn more about you" works surprisingly well with many prospects. What's in it for them? It makes them feel important that you want to learn about them. This feeds their insatiable need for significance.

What we learn from Langer's copy machine study is when we ask people to do something for us, like give up their time, they are more likely to do so when we give them a reason.

The because statement connects the dots between what you want (time) and why they should give it to you. You've interrupted their day, told them why you are calling, and now you must give them a reason to give up more of their precious time to you.

The person you are calling could not care less about your pitch for why you think they should join the military. They don't care about your "blueprinting" or "APPLEMDT" qualifying process. They don't care about what you want or what you would "love" or "like" to do. They don't care about your story.

They only care about what is relevant to their problems, and they will give up their time to you for their reasons, not yours. This is why your message matters. What you say and how you say it will either generate resistance and objections or it will pull the wall down and open the door to a "yes."

Avoid saying things like:

- "I want to talk to you."
- "I'd love to get together with you to show you what we have to offer."
- "I want to tell you about _____."

These statements are all about you and the words *talk*, *tell*, and *show* send a subtle message that what you really want to do is pitch. I assure you, the last thing your prospect wants or has time for is you pitching them.

Instead, craft a short, compelling message that connects emotionally with what is important to your prospect. Use phrases and emotional words like:

- Learn more about you and what you want for your future
- Share some insights that have helped other students in your situation make more informed choices
- Find out about your plans for financing college
- Gain an understanding of your unique situation
- Learn how the military might fit into your vision for the future
- Flexibility
- Options
- Peace of mind
- Save
- Frustrated
- Concerned
- Stressed
- Time
- Money

These statements and words are all about them. Prospects want to feel that you get them and their problems or are at least trying to get them before they'll agree to give up their time for you.

The most effective way to craft the right message is to simply stand in your prospect's shoes. Look at things through their eyes and use your God-given empathy to sense their emotions and consider what might be important to them.

Take a moment now to craft a set of because statements for each type of prospect in Table 15.1.

Table 15.1 Because statements

	Alpha	Student	Grad	Prior Service	Inbound Lead
1					
2					
3					
4					
5					

Ask and Shut Up

The most important step in the process is asking for what you want—confidently, assumptively, and assertively.

- Ask for a day and time for a face-to-face interview or meeting.
- Ask for the information you need in order to qualify the prospect.
- Should you want to engage directly in a recruiting conversation, ask an open-ended question that gets them talking.

Your goal is to get to yes, no, or maybe fast. Don't waste any time here. Don't talk in circles. Don't use passive, limp language and phrases like "maybe if it would be okay and if you are not too busy, we could kinda maybe get together for a few minutes, what do you think?"

Be confident, direct, and smooth—and don't pause. Get to the point. Ask and assume. Then shut up.

The single biggest mistake recruiters make on prospecting calls (phone and in person) is to keep talking instead of giving the prospect the opportunity to respond. This increases resistance, triggers objections, and gives your prospect an easy way out.

So shut up and let your prospect respond. Will you get objections and resistance? Absolutely. This is reality—in recruiting there are always objections. However, because you wasted no time getting to the objection, you will have more time to respond, which in turn will give you a better chance of achieving your objective.

We're going to dive headfirst into techniques for dealing with rejection and getting past reflex responses, brush-offs, and objections in upcoming chapters. What I want to impress upon you, though, is just how many prospects will say yes when you are assertive and confident, and assume through your words and tone of voice that they're going to say yes.

Ask for what you want, and then shut up.

Qualify

The order of the Seven-Step Telephone Prospecting Framework is likely the antithesis of what you were taught in recruiting school and how most recruiters approach telephone prospecting. Instead of qualifying first and then asking for the interview, we are flipping these steps. Once you've gained agreement for the interview, then stop and qualify.

Why do I advise you to gain agreement for the interview first and then qualify—isn't that backwards? Trust me on this one, it's not. Instead, it's in line with how the human brain works.

First, I want you to consider how many times you've qualified a prospect on the phone (Height and weight, check. Medical history, check. Tattoos, check. Criminal history, check)—only to be blindsided later by negative information that did not come out when you initially asked.

This happens because of how the human mind deals with difficult questions, like the ones you ask when qualifying. It's a response called cognitive dissonance, which is painful mental stress caused when we try to hold two opposing values at the same time.

Recruiters trigger cognitive dissonance when they start asking difficult qualifying questions up front.

When you ask your prospect tough qualifying questions, they know that some answers may disqualify them. Since they believe that they are qualified, giving you information that contradicts this belief causes dissonance, so their subconscious conveniently forgets about that time when they were charged with underaged drinking and an open-container violation.

Those questions also cause your prospects to erect an emotional wall—especially if they are with friends, family, or their parents when you call. It's what your reaction would be if a stranger approached you and asked you about your medical and criminal history. You'd immediately put up a wall, begin moving in the opposite direction, or give less than forthright answers. It's only when a relationship and trust have been established that you feel comfortable opening up.

It's no different when you start pounding your prospect with:

- How old are you?
- What is your birthday?
- Where were you born?
- What is your Social Security number?
- Are you a registered voter?
- Do you know your selective service number?
- Have you ever been under the care of a doctor?
- Did you have any childhood illnesses, allergies, injuries, broken bones?
- How about surgeries, such as appendix, tonsils, wisdom teeth removal?
- Do you have tubes in your ears?
- When was the last time you used marijuana or any other drugs?
- How tall are you?
- How much do you weigh?
- Do you have any tattoos or piercings?
- Where are they located on your body?
- Are you now or have you ever been a member of or processed for any branch of the military?

- Have you ever been a member of any youth organization such as JROTC, ROTC, Naval Sea Cadets, Air Force Civil Air Patrol, National Defense Cadets, or the Boy Scouts/Girl Scouts? If so, what awards did you receive?
- Have you ever had any law violations, including traffic tickets? What was the disposition of those cases?
- Are you a high school or college graduate?
- What grade of high school are you in?
- What school do/did you attend?
- How many college credits have you currently earned? How many are you going to complete this semester/year?
- Have you ever been married or divorced? Are you planning to get married or divorced in the near future?
- Is your spouse in the military now?
- Is anyone morally, legally, or financially dependent upon you for support?
- Have you ever taken the Armed Service Vocational Aptitude Battery Test?
- What was your score, and when did you take the test?

It is not unusual to overhear a recruiter pulling on the latex gloves for a complete A-to-Z qualification proctology exam on a prospecting call. This barrage of questions immediately turns your prospect off, causing them to raise their emotional wall and defensiveness. It pushes them away.

"But Jeb, what if they are not qualified? Then it gets awkward telling them that it doesn't make sense to meet."

That's the top question I get from recruiters when we walk them through the Seven-Step Telephone Prospecting Framework. I get it. It requires far less emotional investment to use qualifying questions to talk people out of meeting with you than to connect with them first and be upfront with the truth should there not be a fit. We all have a natural fear of conflict and rejection, and the process of asking for the interview before qualifying seems counterintuitive.

Once recruiters take a leap of faith and leverage the process, though, they experience how brilliantly it works. First, in many cases the prospect will do the work for you and disqualify themselves after you ask for a commitment for the interview time and date. This saves you a ton of time.

Second, when you are kind, polite, and professional, prospects get it when you deliver the message that they are not eligible. They don't fight back when you respectfully tell them the truth. This, by the way, is how you can flip the call into a referral.

What's critical to understand about humans is that the emotional wall comes down and the accuracy of the qualifying information improves once they've already agreed to the interview. Because the hardest ask is for their time, once they make that commitment it's all downhill from there, and they'll be more transparent and open to answering your questions. You experience less resistance and reduce objections because you didn't turn them off up front.

Confirm or Flip the Call into a Referral (if not Qualified)

Once you've qualified your prospect enough for a face-to-face interview, simply confirm the appointment time, date, and place. Ask for an e-mail address and permission to send a reminder text. Tell them exactly what they need to bring to the interview.

If, on the other hand, the prospect is not qualified to advance to an interview, respectfully tell them why and ask if they have friends you should be talking to. You'll be surprised at how often you'll get a referral when you are kind, empathetic, and respectful.

Practice the Framework

The key to mastering the Seven-Step Telephone Prospecting Framework is practice. It's like every other thing you've mastered during your career in the military. Repetition is the mother of skill and builds mental "muscle" memory.

16 | Just Eat the Frog

If it's your job to eat a frog, it's best to do it first thing in the morning. And if it's your job to eat two frogs, it's best to eat the biggest one first.
                                                                    —Mark Twain

The most frequent question I get about telephone prospecting is:

"Jeb, what is the best time to call? I mean, is there a time when people will be more receptive to my calls? You know, like, is it better to contact a prospect during the morning than the end of the day? Or are there some days of the week that are better than others?"

This is followed by a longing expectation that I will reveal the secret code that will open them up to a utopian world where prospects always answer the phone, are always in chipper moods, receptive to recruiting pitches, agree to interviews without rejection, and qualify themselves.

I get this question from recruiters across all branches of the military—all the time. There are several reasons recruiters ask this question:

- They are truly interested in timing their calls more effectively.
- They are frustrated and just venting, in which case my answer falls on deaf ears.
- They are seeking a way out of making calls—an excuse.

Timing calls is the greatest excuse and cop-out for recruiters who don't want to prospect by phone (or frankly, prospect at all).

- "I can't call when people are getting ready for the day because it will disturb them."
- "I can't call in the early morning because people are sleeping."
- "I can't call on Friday because people are getting ready for the weekend and won't be interested in talking."
- "I can't call on the weekend because people are doing things and won't answer my calls."
- "I can't call on Monday because people are starting their week and won't be interested in talking."
- "I can't call during the day because people are at school or at work and don't want to be bothered."
- "I can't call before lunch because people are getting ready to go to lunch."
- "I can't call during lunch because people are eating and I don't want to disturb them."
- "I can't call after lunch because people are just getting back."
- "I can't call in the afternoon because people are involved in after-school activities."
- "I can't call in the evening because people are eating dinner, doing homework, spending time with their families, sleeping."
- "I can't call before school, I can't call during school, and I can't call after school—because, because, because."
- "No worries; I'll just prospect tomorrow when people will be more likely to answer my calls."

The excuses for not calling because the timing is wrong are endless and easy. So telephone prospecting is put off day after day, until the recruiting funnel is dead empty. Then these desperate recruiters end up in front of me looking for the top-secret call-timing technique that will make everything okay.

A great analogy for timing your calls is investing. The investor who attempts to time the market has historically failed to beat the investor who uses a dollar-cost-averaging strategy—making incremental investments on a regular schedule over time.

If you think about prospecting in the same vein, recruiters who prospect daily, on a regular schedule, are always more successful over time than those who try to time their prospecting. As in investing, statistics are always in the favor of the recruiter who does a little bit of prospecting every day. Never, ever underestimate the sheer power of a little bit of action applied every day.

Yes, there are times when your prospects are in school and less likely to answer the phone. However, many will text you back when you call and engage in a conversation with you, right in the middle of the school day. Yes, there are times when your prospects are at work. Despite that, they quite often answer the phone and give you a better time to reach them.

Certainly, it makes sense to schedule call blocks for the morning, afternoon, and evenings to give yourself the greatest statistical probability of reaching prospects. Likewise it's a good idea to schedule blocks on Saturday mornings.

However, after working with recruiters and observing thousands of calls, it is clear to me that all the myths I hear about "the best time to call" are just bunk.

Forget about timing your calls and commit instead to daily prospecting blocks starting with a first-thing-in-the-morning call block. Why? Because when you start your day with prospecting it energizes you, builds your confidence, and helps you feel accomplished. It also means that prospecting will get done. It's about front-loading your day with the most impactful thing you can do as a recruiter—getting prospects in for interviews.

Frenchman Nicholas Chamfort advised people to "swallow a toad in the morning if you want to encounter nothing more disgusting the rest of the day." In his book *Eat That Frog*, Brian Tracy says that your "frog" is "the hardest, most important task of the day. It is the one task that can have the greatest positive impact on your results at the moment."

Prospecting is the most important activity in recruiting. It is the one activity that will have the greatest positive impact on the health of your pipeline. It also sucks. It's frustrating, uncomfortable, and covered with green frog slime.

Staring at the frog will not make it more appetizing. The same with prospecting. Thinking about it, pushing it off, or trying to time it will not make it any more appetizing.

The longer that frog sits there, the fouler it gets. That's when the bargaining begins. Instead of just eating it and getting it over with, you start making deals with yourself to "double up" on your frog eating tomorrow.

It never works. Once you start procrastinating, you'll never catch up. When you push prospecting off, more tasks, problems, and burning fires move in to take its place.

This is why you should block your first hour every day for telephone activity. Set the appointment with yourself and keep it. Your energy level, confidence, and enthusiasm will be at their peak at the beginning of the day. Plus prospects will have fewer things on their plate as they begin their day, which makes for less resistance and more *yeses*.

Embrace the suck and eat that frog.

17 | Leaving Effective Voice Mail Messages That Get Returned

I see people putting text messages on the phone or computer and I think, "Why don't you just call?"

—William Shatner, actor

No matter how proficient you become with the Seven-Step Telephone Prospecting Framework, no matter how targeted your prospecting list or focused your phone block, no matter how well you time your dials, the majority of your calls are still going to go unanswered—many to voice mail.

Of course, in some cases, especially with high-school students, the prospect has not set up a voice mail box. Still, when there is a voice mail box, leaving a message can feel like a waste of time. There are always these little questions floating around in the back of your mind:

When should I leave a voice mail message?

Should I even leave a voice mail message?

If I do leave a message, will I get called back?
What should I say?

While there are no definitive answers to any of these questions, knowing how to leave voice mail messages is important, because prospects do listen to and will return voice mail. It's also true that when you leave a voice mail, and the voice mail alert pops up on your prospect's phone screen, the probability that you will get a call or text message back is much higher than when you don't leave a voice mail.

An effective voice mail should help you achieve at least one of three objectives:

1. Get a call back
2. Get a text message response
3. Build familiarity

But, leaving a voice mail is time inefficient. It takes time to work your way through the phone prompts. At around 30 seconds per voice mail, you can easily spend 10 to 15 minutes of an hour-long phone block just leaving voice mail messages.

The call-back rate on voice mail messages is very low. As in single-digits low. This is why when you leave voice mail, it has to count.

Five-Step Voice Mail Framework to Double Callbacks

As I trudge through my voice mail messages, there are three kinds that drive me crazy:

- **No contact information:** These messages are automatically deleted.
- **Long-winded:** Somewhere in the middle of their droning on and on, I usually hit "delete."
- **Garbled contact information:** When I have to listen to a message more than once, it wastes my time and I delete it.

Figure 17.1   Five-Step Voice Mail Framework

Here's the deal: To get more of your messages returned, you must make it easier for your prospects to call you back. There are five steps to leaving effective voice mail messages that get returned (see Figure 17.1). When you deploy this process consistently, you will double your callback rate.

1. **Identify yourself.** Say who you are—rank, name, branch— right up front. This makes you sound professional.
2. **Say your phone number twice.** Prospects can't call back if they don't hear or can't understand your number. Give your contact information up front and say it twice—slowly. In some cases, after they hear your name and military branch, they may not care about the rest of your message because based on their situation, they can infer why you are calling, and they'll call you back. Finally, because voice mail to text translation is becoming more common, your phone number ends up at the top of the translation, and a quick click on the link dials you right up.
3. **Tell them the reason for your call.** Tell them why you have called. After you give your personal information just say, "The reason for my call is to schedule an interview," or "The purpose of my call is to invite you to our next event." Tell them why you are calling and what you want. Transparency is both respectful and professional.
4. **Give them a compelling reason to call you back.** Prospects call back when you have something that they want or are curious about. Curiosity is a powerful driver of behavior. When you have knowledge, insight, incentives, urgency, or even "want to learn more about" them, you create a motivating force that compels your prospect to call you back.

5. **Repeat your name and say your phone number twice.** Before you end your message, say your name again slowly and clearly and always, *always* say your number twice. This way your prospect doesn't need to go back to the beginning and listen to your number again—thus making it easy for them to return your call.

Bonus tip: Keep voice mail messages to 30 seconds. When you hold yourself to 30 seconds, you are forced to be clear, succinct, and professional.

> Hi, Marie, this is Sergeant Sweyer with the United States Marines. My phone number is 1-888-360-2249, that's 1-888-360-2249. The reason I am calling is you filled out a form indicating that you were interested in learning more about career opportunities with the Marines and I want to schedule an interview to learn more about you and find out if you qualify for the new signing incentives that just became available to me. Let's get together this week. Give me a call back at 1-888-360-2249, that's 1-888-360-2249.

I am aware that it feels awkward to say your phone number four times on the same voice mail message. Your goal is to make it easy for your prospect to call you back, not more comfortable for you.

By hearing your phone number twice up front, they don't need to listen to the entire message to get your phone number if they are ready to call you back. If your message intrigued them and they want to call you back, you also gave them your number twice at the end, so they don't have to replay the message. Making it easy increases the probability that you'll get a call or text back.

Develop Compelling Voice Mail Messages

Take a few minutes now to develop a set of compelling reasons to call you back for each category of prospect. Record them in Table 17.1.

Table 17.1 **Compelling reasons to call back**

	Alpha	Student	Grad	Prior Service	Inbound Lead
1					
2					
3					
4					
5					

PART VII

Objections

18

Objections Are Not Rejection, but They Feel That Way

I believe that rejection is a blessing because it's the universe's way of telling you that there's something better out there.
                                    —Michelle Phan, makeup artist

For a high-school junior, the prom was a big deal—an obsession for teenaged boys and girls and one of the big steps out of adolescence and into adulthood. I was excited and yet worried, because I had a big problem. I needed a date. And, of course, I wanted to go with the girl of my dreams.

The anxiety I felt was the same anxiety that millions of high-school students have endured—a rite of passage. For weeks, I put off asking her. I watched her in the lunchroom huddled with her friends. I passed her in the hall between classes, secretly hoping that she was thinking the same thing I was.

There was never a good time. I couldn't get her alone, didn't have the right words. Other people were around. I had a hundred-and-one reasons why *now* wasn't the right time to ask.

So, for most of the winter semester, I lived in the fantasy that we were going to the prom together rather than taking the most important step and *asking* her. With the clock ticking, though, I needed to do something.

Finally, I gathered up my courage and asked. It was a terrifying experience. I felt self-conscious and insecure as I struggled to get the words out. My heart was pounding and palms sweating. As soon as I opened my mouth, I regretted it.

The words I'd practiced over and over in my head came out wrong—an embarrassing jumbled mess. In that instant, my dream of going to the prom with "the most beautiful girl at my school" was dashed. It was over, and I knew it.

I was already walking away when she said *yes*. In retreat mode, I was so consumed by fear and embarrassment that I didn't comprehend at first. Everything turned around, though, on that beautiful, miraculous, improbable *yes!*

I felt as if I'd won an Olympic gold medal. She said yes, and suddenly everything in my 16-year-old life was perfect. I was going to the prom with an A-list date. The stress and anxiety had been lifted.

I rented my tux, made dinner reservations, scheduled a limo, and arranged for a corsage. For three weeks, I was as happy as I'd ever been.

Then suddenly, without warning, it all came crashing down. While I was walking down the hall to my next class, one of my date's friends handed me a note (this was before text messaging). I eagerly opened it. But the words on the paper smashed into me like a ton of bricks. I just stood there staring at the note, stunned.

My worst nightmare. My date had a change of heart and decided not to go to the prom with me. She'd found a better escort—an old boyfriend who'd conveniently come back into the picture right before the prom.

It's difficult to describe the emotions I was feeling at the time, but I remember it as if a bomb had gone off. My ears were ringing, vision blurred, and I stumbled through the remainder of the day dazed and numb.

I was embarrassed, ashamed, hurt, and angry. I wanted to confront her, to tell her how wrong she was to do this, but I didn't. I just folded up like a cheap lawn chair, went home, and licked my wounds. I still had time to find another date, but I was so stung it wasn't in me to ask anyone else. I didn't go to my junior prom—something I regret to this day. Instead I hid out at home and felt like a loser.

This awful experience was pure, unadulterated *rejection*. It left a scar so deep that I've never told this story until now. Even my wife had never heard it. It still hurts. Rejection feels deeply personal.

Not the Same

Objections are not rejection. When prospects, parents, and educators push back on your requests for meetings, information, and access, their objections are signs of confusion, concerns, the sorting out of options, subconscious cognitive biases, risk aversion, cognitive overload, and the fear of change.

Objections are a natural part of the human decision-making process. In most cases, objections are a sign that your prospect is still engaged.

Questions are not rejection. Prospects, their parents, and people in their circle of influence often ask legitimate but tough questions that they need answered before moving forward.

Negotiation is not rejection. Negotiation is a clear indication that your prospect is engaged and ready to enlist; the door is open to collaborate on a mutually beneficial offer, timing, MOS, or incentive package.

Objections, questions, and negotiation sounds like this:

"I don't know; I'm going to need to think about it." (Objection)

"I need to run this by my parents (wife, husband, friend, coach, etc.)." (Objection)

"Before moving forward, I'm going to need to look at all of my options." (Objection)

"I don't have time right now." (Objection)

"I'm not interested." (Objection)

"The military is not for me." (Objection)

"I don't want my kid to get killed. (Objection)

"I'm already going to college." (Objection)

"I think I can make more money in a civilian job." (Objection)

"What MOS will I qualify for?" (Question)

"Will I be deployed overseas?" (Question)

"Why does it work this way instead of that way?" (Question)

"How is your branch different from the others?" (Question)

"I want to wait until after graduation to go to MEPS." (Negotiation)

"I want to join, but I want to wait until next summer to go to basic." (Negotiation)

Rejection is the outright refusal to accept an idea or request. It is a flat *no* that at times may be delivered with a harsh and deliberate tone. In rare cases, rejection is hurled at you as a personal insult.

Rejection sounds like this:

"Get the hell out of my house, you baby killer!" (Rejection!)

"Take me off your f@#!ing list and don't ever call me again!" (Rejection!)

"You suck!" (Rejection!)

"I wouldn't enlist with you if you were the last person on earth!" (Rejection!)

"Go screw yourself!" (Rejection!)

Click or slam—phone being hung up or door being shut in your face. (Rejection!)

"Get out of my classroom now!" (Rejection!)

"We don't want you in our school." (Rejection!)

In recruiting, the most blatant, personal, and harsh rejections occur during prospecting activity at the top of the funnel, when you are interrupting strangers and asking for time.

But It Feels the Same

There is a big, big difference between an objection, a question, or a negotiation, and *rejection*. A big difference. The problem is, in the moment of silence after you've asked for something, when your emotions are reeling, it can be difficult to tell the difference.

At the purely emotional level, rejection and objections can and often do feel the same. This is because rejection can be:

- **Real:** Actual rejection.
- **Anticipated:** Worrying about the potential for rejection can kick off a wave of disruptive emotions.
- **Perceived:** Mistaking an objection, a question, or an attempt to negotiate for real rejection can produce a natural emotional and neurophysiological response that feels like being rejected.

It is the anticipation or perception of rejection that makes an objection feel as if it is real rejection.

Of course, I could attempt to rationalize this with you, just as I did in the previous section, by illustrating the difference between an objection and a rejection. In training rooms across the military, this is exactly what is done. Trainers address recruiting objections with an appeal to the rational part of your brain. They admonish you not to take objections personally—to just let them roll off your back.

Likewise, leaders pound on the table and tell you to toughen up or tap out. But this noise is mostly ineffective. If telling recruiters to suck it up and not take objections personally worked, we'd all be champions at asking for what we want and getting past *no*.

I believe it is completely disingenuous to tell you that you can just snap your fingers, detach from rejection, and let it roll off your back.

There is no doubt that you can become inspired and motivated enough to run headlong into rejection after hearing a motivational speech or strong message. The problem is that this type of motivation is temporary at best.

When you are out in the community on your own, without sustainable techniques for gaining control over your disruptive emotions, you'll rapidly revert to a more natural state in which you meander around the outskirts of rejection or avoid it altogether—and stop asking.

Trainers say things like, "Just let it roll off your back" because it's easier to offer platitudes and intellectualize the pain of rejection (real, anticipated, or perceived) than to acknowledge that these emotions *are real* and to teach people how to deal with them.

Talking at you about why you shouldn't take objections personally doesn't remove or negate the emotional pain you *actually* feel. Unless you are an emotionless psychopath, rejection hurts and objections sting. Especially when it comes from the very people you've put your life on the line to protect.

The real truth, which no one ever tells you, is the pain you feel in response to rejection—anticipated, perceived, or real—is as much *biological* as it is emotional.

The rub is, you may be able to avoid this pain in the short term by steering clear of anything that even feels like rejection. But by doing so, you'll only hurt yourself, add more stress to your life, and let down your team and ultimately your country.

To be successful, you're going to need to ask for what you want and learn strategies for dealing with the repercussions.

- The first step on this journey begins with gaining a clear understanding of the origins of the fear of rejection and an awareness of how it manifests itself and holds you back.
- The next step is developing self-awareness of your own disruptive emotions and emotional triggers.
- Finally, you must master a framework that gives you the power to rise above your emotions in the moment, get past prospecting objections, and achieve your desired outcome.

19 | The Science Behind the Hurt

We shouldn't romanticize rejection. There's nothing romantic about rejection. It's horrible.

—Marlon James, Jamaican novelist

The genesis of much of our behavior—good and bad, destructive and effective—lies outside the reaches of our conscious minds. We act but are unaware of why we act unless we choose to tune in and become aware.

Awareness is the intentional and deliberate choice to monitor, evaluate, and modulate your emotions so that your responses to the people and environment around you are congruent with your intentions and objectives. Awareness of why you *fear* rejection begins with an intellectual understanding of the science behind the hurt.

I want you to image that you were alive 40,000 years ago. You live in a cave with a group of people as part of a hunter-gatherer community, in what is now France. It's a dangerous world. Neighboring tribes fight and compete for scarce resources. When you are out hunting for dinner, there is usually something hunting you. It's a brutal, survival-of-the-fittest environment.

You depend on your tribe for everything. You cannot survive on your own. Should you get kicked out of the cave into the dark, you would have no fire, no food, no protection, and no companionship. Essentially, it's a death sentence. It's a world that's hard to imagine in our tech-dominated modern society, where food, shelter, transportation, and even companionship is at our fingertips with a click or swipe on our smartphone screens.

It was here, in this ruthless and unforgiving ancient world, that humans developed sensitivity to rejection. The pain of rejection served as an early warning system that you were running into imminent danger of being ostracized or banished if your behavior did not change. It was a simple, but powerful, survival mechanism.

Humans who developed sensitivity to the pain of rejection were able to function more effectively in groups. They were more likely to survive and pass on their DNA. Thus, the fear of rejection became a competitive evolutionary advantage.

Over the course of human history, banishment was considered worse than death. The stories in ancient literature often depicted it as such. Though today banishment is far from a death sentence, this same emotional dynamic is at play within groups of humans. Rejection remains a painful emotion that teaches us how to act and conform to group norms.

A Biological Response

This also explains why humans find it easier to remember and re-experience rejection than other emotions or even physical pain. Your brain prioritizes the pain of rejection because remembering this pain warns you not to repeat socially damaging mistakes and face the scorn of your neighbors.

It's the vivid re-experiencing that makes rejection unique among human emotions. Whenever you bring up the memory of a past rejection, you'll find it easy to reactivate and relive the same painful feelings you had at the time. The same is not true for other emotions. You may remember them, but it is difficult to relive them.

This is why it's so difficult for me to discuss my high school prom and why the memory of rejection (perceived or real) causes recruiters to lose their confidence to ask.

Rejection is different from other emotions. While the menagerie of emotions you feel originate and live in the emotional hub of your brain (called the limbic system), rejection activates the areas of your brain connected to physical pain. Rejection, unlike every other emotion, mimics physical pain,[1] which explains why it hurts so much. Scientists have even discovered that taking Tylenol reduces the pain of rejection, while it has no impact on other emotions.[2]

Fear of rejection evolved as a biological response in humans because it was so vital to our survival. But the existence of this fear creates a paradox. It is both a powerful teacher and debilitating force that can destroy your dreams.

In effect, it is a double-edged sword. On one hand, it helps you become socially adept so that you may coexist with other human beings. On the other, it triggers waves of disruptive emotions that impede your ability to achieve your goals.[3] Nowhere is this truer than in military recruiting.

The Most Insatiable Human Need

Every human being has an insatiable need to feel important—to know that we matter and belong. This need to feel important is the singularity of human behavior. Everything we do—good and bad—revolves around this insatiable need.

It is this need to feel accepted that makes rejection such a powerful emotional destabilizer. When you get rejected, suddenly you feel alone—disconnected. You believe you are the only person who feels this pain. Your self-talk turns negative. You begin to attack your self-worth and destroy your self-esteem, breeding insecurity. Your emotional desire to belong grows more acute, feeding the disruptive emotions of attachment and desperation.

In this sad downward spiral, you become irrational, and your disruptive emotions only serve to generate even more rejection.[4] This, in turn, leads to depression, sadness, jealousy, isolation, envy, guilt, embarrassment, and anxiety. Judgment and situational awareness suffer.

Inside this emotional storm, you may even become angry and lash out at other people.[5] Innumerable studies have shown that people who have been rejected, even mildly, have a disturbing tendency to take out their aggression on other people, including innocent bystanders. Even the surgeon general of the United States has issued a report on rejection's impact on adolescent violence.

In studies where participants are rejected by strangers but later told that the strangers were just researchers and the rejection wasn't real, the participants still felt rejected. In other experiments, even when participants were told that the person who rejected them was a member of a reviled and despised group like the KKK, they continued to feel the sting of rejection.[6]

These studies illustrate the biggest problem with rejection. It cannot be rationalized; it doesn't respond to reason. That's why telling you not to take it personally doesn't work.

20 | Rejection Proof

No one can make you feel inferior without your consent.
—Eleanor Roosevelt

Imagine that you're sitting at home when suddenly the doorbell rings. You weren't expecting a visitor.

You begin running through a series of images in your mind of who might be at your door—salesperson, Jehovah's Witnesses, Girl Scouts, neighbor, UPS, FedEx? You may fear the worst and imagine that it's a criminal who wants to rob you.

With a measure of curiosity and trepidation, you open the door. But it's not any of the things you imagined. There, standing before you, is a well-groomed young Chinese man wearing soccer cleats.

With suspicion in your voice you ask, "May I help you?"

Sporting a big grin, he responds, "Yes, I came by to ask if you would take a video of me playing soccer in your backyard."

Pause for a moment and consider how you might react to such a strange and unexpected request. Then step into the other person's shoes and imagine what it would be like to be the requester. Both parties, in this weird moment, would be swept up by a sea of disruptive emotions.

This, by the way, is a true story. It's how Jia Jiang became rejection proof.[1] We'll come back to Jia Jiang later in the chapter. First let's consider some basic facts:

- When you became a military recruiter, you are signed up to seek out rejection.
- Seeking out rejection is not natural for humans.
- To build an effective recruiting funnel, you must interrupt strangers.
- To get what you want, you must ask for what you want.
- When you ask, people are going to tell you no.
- The only way to avoid hearing no is to never ask.
- Therefore, to be successful you must gain the discipline to ask and the skills for getting past no.
- Objections are not rejection, but they feel like rejection.
- Rejection triggers your fight-or-flight response and releases a wave of disruptive emotions: fear, insecurity, doubt, and attachment.
- These emotions happen without your consent and can derail you in recruiting conversations.
- In recruiting conversations, whoever exerts the greatest amount of emotional control has the highest probability of getting the outcome they desire.
- Therefore, to bend the probability of a win in your favor, you must rise above and control your disruptive emotions.

The Seven Disruptive Emotions

Disruptive emotions manifest themselves in destructive behaviors that fog focus, cloud situational awareness, cause irrational decision making, lead to misjudgments, and erode confidence.

These seven disruptive emotions impede your ability to get past no:

1. **Fear** is the root cause of most failures in recruiting. It causes you to hesitate and make excuses rather than confidently and assertively ask for what you want. Fear holds you back from prospecting, clouds objectivity, and breeds insecurity.
2. **Desperation** is a disruptive emotion that causes you to become needy and weak, be illogical, and make poor decisions. Desperation makes you instantly unlikable and unattractive to other people, kicking off a vicious cycle that generates even more rejection. Desperation is the mother of insecurity.
3. **Insecurity** drowns confidence and assertiveness. It causes you to feel alone—as if you and only you have a big sign on your back that says "reject me." Insecurity causes you to feel as if rejection is lurking around every corner, so you become gun-shy—afraid of your own shadow.
4. **Need for significance** is a core human desire and weakness. As humans, we all have an insatiable need to be accepted and feel like we matter. When this need gets out of control, it can become one of our most disruptive emotions. Rejection naturally causes you to feel unaccepted and unimportant. Your ego-centric need for significance treats rejection as a threat, thus triggering the fight-or-flight response and causing irrational behavior. The insatiable need for significance is the mother of attachment and eagerness.
5. **Attachment** causes you to become emotionally focused on winning, getting what you want, looking good in front of others, wanting everyone to agree with you, and always being right. As a result you lose perspective and objectivity. Attachment is the enemy of self-awareness and the genesis of delusion.
6. **Eagerness** causes you to become so focused on pleasing other people that you lose sight of your recruiting objectives. You give in and give up too soon. You waste time with applicants who will never qualify or be eligible to join the military.
7. **Worry** is the downside of your brain's vigilant crusade to keep you safe and alive. Your brain naturally focuses on the negatives—what could go wrong—rather than what could

go right. This, in and of itself, can trigger the fight-or-flight response and the stream of disruptive emotions that come with it—based only on *your* perception that something might go wrong. This leads to paralysis from analyzing every negative possibility and avoidance through procrastination.

In concert or individually, these disruptive emotions can lead to dangerous confirmation bias. This human cognitive shortcut causes you to put on rose-colored lenses and see only those things that support your delusional view of the situation (such as excuses for why you missed mission, chased an unqualified prospect, failed to get past an objection, or tanked a parental meeting).

Recruiters who cannot regulate disruptive emotions get caught up in and controlled by emotional waves, much like a rudderless ship tossed at sea in a violent storm—pushed from wave to wave, highs and lows, at whim.

Managing your disruptive emotions is a primary meta-skill of military recruiting. Getting past "no" begins with self-control. The combination of situational awareness and the ability to consistently regulate disruptive emotions is at the heart of confidently approaching prospects, asking for what you want, and mastering objections.

When you learn how to manage your disruptive emotions, you gain the power to influence the emotions of other people at that crucial inflection point when an objection is on the table.

But let's not sweep under the rug just how difficult it is to manage disruptive emotions appropriately in the moment. As humans, we have all been that rudderless ship, helplessly rocked by out-of-control emotions. We've all said or done things in the moment that in retrospect we regretted. We've all avoided the truth. We've all been hit with a hard objection and then stammered and stuttered, searching for the right words in the throes of the fight-or-flight response.

We have all been there, because we are all human.

It is easy to talk about managing disruptive emotions in dispassionate clichés like "just let it roll off your back," but it's an entirely different thing to quell your emotions and turn around an objection when everything inside you just wants to run. Intellect, rational thinking, and process drown in the sea of disruptive emotions and subconscious human instincts.

Develop Self-Awareness

You become rejection proof when you learn to master your emotions. This begins with awareness that the emotion is happening, which allows your rational brain to take the helm, make sense of the emotion, rise above it, and choose your behavior and response.

Much of our behavior begins outside the reaches of our conscious minds. We act but are unaware of why we act, unless we choose to tune in and become aware. Awareness is the intentional and deliberate choice to monitor, evaluate, and modulate emotions so that our emotional responses to the people and environment around us are congruent with our intentions and objectives.

Remember Jia Jiang from the opening story in this chapter? Intentional awareness is how he became rejection proof.

Jiang intentionally sought out rejection by coming up with ridiculous and terrifying requests of strangers. At each step, he videoed his physical response to rejection and recounted his emotional response on a public blog. As he faced each new rejection and monitored his response, he became more aware of his emotions—how he felt before, during, and after.

Jia Jiang learned that there is a difference between experiencing emotions and being caught up in them. Awareness helped him gain control over his emotions. While buffeted by the emotional storms that were activated by the rejection he sought out, Jiang learned to make conscious, rational choices with his reactions.

Awareness begins with learning to anticipate the anxiety that comes right before asking for what you want. Once you gain this insight, practice intentionally managing your internal self-talk and physical reactions to that fear. Focus on rising above your emotions and becoming a detached, dispassionate observer.

Self-awareness is the doorway to emotional control. Awareness helps you manage your outward physiology despite the volcanic emotions that may be erupting below the surface. Like a duck on the water, you appear calm and cool and project a relaxed, confident demeanor on the outside even though you're paddling frantically just below the surface.

Positive Visualization

Your brain is hardwired to anticipate and dwell on worst-case scenarios. When you face an emotionally unpleasant task, it is human nature to begin fabricating negative outcomes in your head. Without rational intervention, these internal narratives can lead to self-fulfilling prophesies.

For instance, Petty Officer Second Class Martinez expects to encounter resistance on a prospecting call. This negative visualization makes her feel insecure. Lacking confidence, she approaches the call with trepidation. When the prospect answers, she stumbles over her words, sounding weak. The prospect bulldozes over her. Martinez is shaken and expects she'll get even more resistance on her next call. Now even more insecure, she attracts rejection like a magnet.

"Because the brain's focus on threat and danger far outperforms the reward capacities of the brain, it is important to keep a deliberate eye on positive possibilities," advises Scott Halford in his book *Activate Your Brain*.[2] Had Martinez approached the call with confidence, her demeanor alone would have reduced resistance and generated a more positive outcome.

It is for this reason that elite athletes[3] and elite military recruiters employ visualization to preprogram the subconscious brain. When you visualize success, you teach your mind to act in a way that helps your achieve your desired outcome.[4]

Begin by focusing on your breathing. Slow it down. Then in your mind's eye, go through each part of the call step by step. Focus on how it feels to be confident. Imagine what you will say, what you will ask. Visualize yourself succeeding. Repeat this process again and again until you've trained your mind to manage the disruptive emotions that derail you.

Manage Self-Talk

Sometimes (especially when prospecting), no matter how nice or professional you are, the person you are calling on will tell you to "go screw yourself," scream "Don't ever call me again," or say "It will be a cold day in hell before I ever join the military!" They may slam the door in your face, ask you to leave the building, or respond harshly to your e-mail or text message.

Sometimes prospects are rude, short-tempered, and curt; they take shots at you that are pointed and personal. Sometimes it's because you caught them at a bad time. Sometimes you're just a convenient human piñata for their frustrations and self-loathing.

When you are treated this way, it's natural to dwell on it and replay the conversation again and again in your head. You feel embarrassed, angry, and vengeful, along with a host of other disruptive emotions.

You project your emotions on your prospects and make up a story in your head about what they said, did, or thought after they hung up the phone, pressed send in response to your e-mail, or kicked you out of their door. You see your prospects laughing at you or fuming because you annoyed them.

Meanwhile, the prospect doesn't even remember you. They moved on the moment you hung up the phone and haven't given you another thought. You were just a blip—a momentary and meaningless interruption in their day.

It is difficult to regain your focus and keep moving when a prospect is rude to you. It hurts. It's all you can think about. You fantasize about calling back and telling them to F@*K OFF! Anger invades your thoughts, keeps you stewing, and derails your recruiting day.

According to Amanda Chan, citing the research of psychologist Guy Winch, "Many times the rejection does 50 percent of the damage and we do the other 50 percent of the damage."[5] The greatest injury from rejection is self-inflicted. Just when our self-esteem is hurting most, we go and make it worse.

There is an endless and ongoing stream of chatter inside your head, shaping your emotions and outward actions. The conversation you are having with yourself will either build your attitude, strengthen your belief system, and generate a winning mind-set or trigger disruptive emotions that destroy you.

Unlike emotions, which are activated without your consent, *self-talk* is completely within your control. *You* make the choice to think positively or negatively. To pick yourself up or tear yourself down. To see a glass half-full or half-empty. To be aware or delusional.

Sit quietly and listen to the conversation in your head—the words you are using, the questions you are asking. Then resolve to change those words so they support the image of who you want to be, how you want to act, and how you want to feel. Make an intentional decision to remain tuned in to your inner voice. When it goes negative, stop and change the conversation.

One way to do this is to develop a bounce-back routine. Find something that gets you pumped up and helps you get your confidence back after you've been rejected. This could be an inspirational quote, an affirmation, a friend you call, music you listen to, or exercise. Develop a routine that snaps you out of your funk quickly.

Over the years I've developed a simple routine that gets me back on track when a prospect hits me with hard rejection. Behind my desk is an old index card taped to the wall. The paper has yellowed, and the words have faded just a bit because I've carried that card around with me for 25 years. On the card are four letters:

N-E-X-T

Change Your Physiology

Studies on human behavior from virtually every corner of the academic world have proven time and again that we can change how we feel by adjusting our physical posture. In other words, internal emotions may be shaped by your outward physiology.

When you anticipate being rejected, you tend to slump your shoulders, lower your chin, and look at the floor—physical signals of insecurity and emotional weakness. This change in physical posture makes you appear less confident to others and feel less confident on the inside.

A change in physical posture not only elicits a change in emotions,[6] but it also triggers a neurophysiological response.[7] We know, for example, that the hormones cortisol and testosterone play a significant role in creating the feeling of confidence.

Research by Amy Cuddy of Harvard University demonstrates that "power posing," physically standing in a posture of confidence, even when you don't feel confident, impacts testosterone and cortisol levels in the brain, influencing confidence.[8]

Moms, teachers, coaches, and drill instructors have always known this basic truth. They've been giving us this same advice for years. Keep your chin up. Stand at attention. Straighten your shoulders. Sit up straight and you'll feel better.

When you put your shoulders up and chin up, you look and feel confident. In uniform, you feel more confident. Use assertive and assumptive words, phrases, and voice tone, and you will be more powerful and credible—and more likely to get a "yes" when you ask for what you want.

Stay Fit

As soon as you let your guard down, your emotions begin to run amok at your expense—especially when you are tired, hungry, and physically exhausted.

Regulating and managing disruptive emotions is draining. Moving past the emotional hurdle of rejection requires a tremendous amount of mental energy, but your mental energy is limited by your physical resilience.

Military recruiters spend an inordinate amount of time driving, sitting, and staring at screens. Sitting all day while staring at a screen impacts your mental capacity and slows both your mental and physical responses in emotionally charged situations.

Staying fit improves self-esteem, creative thinking, mental clarity, confidence, and optimism. It makes you more nimble and adaptive and helps you gain the discipline to maintain emotional self-control. When you remain physically fit, you also become emotionally fit. An avalanche of scientific research proves that physical resilience leads to mental and emotional resilience.

In the fast-paced, stressful world of military recruiting, it can be difficult to eat well. Eating poorly is like putting low-grade gasoline in a high-performance race car. To gain the mental toughness and resiliency to control your emotions, you need to fill up with high-test fuel.

Filling up early is the key—starting with breakfast. It's easy to skip meals when you are in a hurry, but allowing yourself to get hungry is a big, big mistake. You lose intellectual acuity and emotional control when you are hungry.

Nothing impacts your ability to deal confidently with objections more than sleep. Sleep deprivation has a profound impact on your cognitive ability and degrades your emotional intelligence. You become susceptible to breaks in emotional discipline.

Humans need between seven and nine hours of sleep every night for optimal performance. These days, though, it has become a badge of honor to live on little sleep. Arianna Huffington, the cofounder and editor-in-chief of the *Huffington Post*, opines that "we are in the midst of a sleep deprivation crisis. Only by renewing our relationship with sleep can we take back control of our lives."

All sorts of bad things happen to you when you are not getting enough sleep. Over the long term, you become more susceptible to immune deficiencies, obesity, heart disease, and mood disorders, and your life expectancy is reduced. "Living with the mindset 'I'll sleep when I'm dead' may get you there quite a bit faster!" says Joe De Sena in his book *Spartan Up!: A Take-No-Prisoners Guide to Overcoming Obstacles and Achieving Peak Performance in Life*.

Obstacle Immunity

"So, wait a minute. Let me get this right. You would rather go into battle and be shot at by people who are trying to kill you than pick up the phone and make a prospecting call to a teenager." I looked out on the faces and saw the truth there.

The noncommissioned officers, all of whom were wearing combat patches, nodded and laughed as they acknowledged the uncomfortable truth. I was laughing too but stunned by their response. It was the moment I decided to write this book.

As I dived deeper into military recruiting, I learned that most military recruiters who struggle to make mission aren't failing because they lack knowledge, talent, passion, and experience or because they are lazy. They fail because of a daunting emotional obstacle. They fear rejection and therefore don't ask for what they want assumptively, assertively, and confidently.

On the other hand, for me, making prospecting calls to teenagers is easy—far easier than cold-calling businesses as I've done my entire career. In my view, I'm doing them a favor—giving them a job, college tuition, and amazing benefits. I've got a bag full of money that I'm going to give to somebody. "Who wants it?" That's my mind-set. But then again, I've made thousands of prospecting calls over the past 25 years.

It seemed completely irrational that these brave men and women, who had endured the hyperemotional environment of an active battlefield where death is around every corner, would be afraid of getting rejected by teenagers. On the surface, it made no logical sense that they'd rather face bullets than potential rejection.

When I even consider running into a hail of bullets, it elicits fear. Going into battle versus interrupting a stranger? I'll gladly face the rejection. After all, I can't think of anyone who's gotten PTSD from prospecting.

The soldiers in my classroom, though, could only see rejection. Cold-calling prospects in an environment that they could not control and did not understand created what felt like an insurmountable obstacle. And there is a good reason why they felt this way.

The military prepares you before sending you into war zones. You learn to manage your natural fight-or-flight response and race headlong into dangerous situations that would cause most people to freeze or run—potentially getting other people killed.

Before sending you into combat, the military puts you through endless live-fire drills and mock combat situations. This training conditions you to control your emotions in battle. You learn battle rhythm, operational frameworks, and ways to respond. You learn "ledges" (we'll discuss this further in an upcoming chapter) for getting in control of runaway emotions. You drill and drill until these responses are rote and you become immune to fear in battle.

For my combat veterans, who freely admitted that they avoid prospecting at all costs, the light bulb came on when I drew the parallel between how they learned to be immune to the obstacle of fear on the battlefield and how they could apply the same methodology for becoming immune to the fear of rejection when prospecting. It's simply a shift in perspective.

An obstacle is defined as something that obstructs or hinders progress—a difficulty, problem, or challenge that's in your way.[9]

During World War II, Lawrence Holt, who owned a merchant shipping line in Britain, made an observation that launched a movement. His ships were being targeted and torpedoed by German U-boats. Strangely, the survivors of these attacks were more likely to be old sailors, not younger, more physically fit men.

This phenomenon led Holt to turn to Kurt Hahn, a German educator who had criticized Hitler and been imprisoned by the Nazis for it before the war. Holt engaged Hahn to help him understand why the younger, stronger, more physically fit members of his crews died at an alarmingly higher rate following attacks.

What Holt and Hahn eventually concluded was the difference between the two groups came down to emotional resilience, self-reliance, and inner strength. Even though the younger men possessed superior physical strength and agility, the emotional resilience of the older, more experienced sailors helped them to endure grueling obstacles and survive.

Holt is famous for saying, "I would rather entrust the lowering of a lifeboat in mid-Atlantic to a sail-trained octogenarian than to a young sea technician who is completely trained in the modern way but has never been sprayed by salt water."

The findings led Hahn to found Outward Bound,[10] an organization that has been helping people ever since to develop mental strength, confidence, tenacity, perseverance, resilience, and obstacle immunity by immersing them in harsh conditions.

Remember Jia Jiang? He had hit rock-bottom. His dream of becoming an entrepreneur had been torpedoed by his deep fear of and aversion to rejection. Embarrassed, depressed, and feeling alone, he had an epiphany. His only hope for achieving his dream was to face rejection head-on. This is when Jiang's improbable journey through 100 days of rejection began.

Jiang chronicles how he systematically exposed himself to all levels of rejection in his inspiring book *Rejection Proof*. By asking for money, custom doughnuts, temporary jobs, "burger refills" at a hamburger joint, and the chance to play soccer in a stranger's backyard—among dozens of other strange requests—he got nose-to-nose with emotional obstacles that would make the average human squirm.

At first, he challenged himself with relatively easy asks, then made progressively bigger, more complex requests. It was this progressive exposure to potential, perceived, and actual rejection that helped him become immune to his greatest obstacle—the fear of asking for what he wanted.

Joe De Sena's Spartan Races are designed for the very same purpose—to build obstacle immunity. Participants are pitted against challenging and painful tests of will. Through adversity and suffering, participants learn how to change their mental state and gain control of fear.[11]

Self-control in the face of obstacles is like a muscle. The more you exercise it, the stronger it becomes. You build your "self-control muscle" by putting yourself in position to experience the perceived obstacle and the accompanying emotions again and again.

Once you begin intentionally facing fears and emotionally uncomfortable situations, you learn to disrupt and neutralize the anxiety that comes right before the obstacle. You'll begin shifting your internal self-talk and outward physical reaction to control that fear. Soon overcoming once "insurmountable" obstacles becomes routine.

It's clear as you read Jiang's story that much of his success was created through a mind-set shift that occurred as he gained obstacle immunity. He developed an emotional callus that made it harder for rejection to pierce his thickened skin. As he committed to his rejection challenges and persevered through the fear, he became rejection proof.

Adversity Is Your Most Powerful Teacher

Data from research studies indicate that when your self-esteem and confidence are low, rejection feels more painful and becomes an even greater obstacle.[12] Sadly, in this emotional state you become even more susceptible to rejection.

Most people would agree that my previous statement is a blinding flash of the obvious and a self-evident truth. The problem is that it's not so obvious when you are the person suffering from low self-esteem. When insecurity consumes you, it is very, very difficult to see the negative impacts. You may know rationally that you just need to get back on the horse, but emotionally it feels impossible to face the obstacle again.

As a corollary, people with higher self-esteem are much more resilient in the face of rejection. As Jiang progressed through his 100 days of rejection, he began getting improbable yeses. These wins boosted his self-esteem and his confidence, leading to more wins.

This is where the magic happened. His confidence made it harder for people to say "no," which in turn improved his probability of getting a yes. His newly found self-awareness gave him greater emotional control, which further improved his probability of getting a win.

Outward Bound, Spartan Races, military training, and Jia Jiang all deploy a similar formula for developing obstacle immunity. Participants are pushed through a gauntlet of progressively more difficult and fear-inducing challenges until everything else seems easy in comparison. It is here that emotional resilience is born.

Leveraging Adversity

To become rejection proof, you must be ready and open to learning and gaining resilience through the crucible of adversity and pain.

- You must choose to intentionally face your fear—obstacle immunity is a choice.
- You must actively seek out rejection by asking for what you want.
- You must push through a state of cognitive dissonance in which you cope with the emotional pain of perceived, potential, and real rejection while fighting the desire to go back to your old state of comfort and delusion.

After you push through dissonance and pain, on the other side you'll gain a sense of mastery and confidence. This leads to higher self-esteem and improved performance.

Obstacle immunity means having the mental toughness and attention control to reach peak performance while maintaining a positive mind-set, no matter when adversity presents itself. In other words, no matter what your prospect says, objections cease to faze you. You bounce back quickly, deploy turn-around frameworks effortlessly, and move on to the next call when things don't go your way.

Remember my prom story from earlier in the book? After going through the pain and indignity of getting dumped by my prom date, I vowed that it wouldn't happen again. The easy decision would have been to skip the prom my senior year. No request, no rejection—easy. But I wanted to go to my senior prom, and I knew who I wanted to go with. That was enough motivation to find the courage to do it again.

This time, though, I took no chances. Rather than waiting until the last minute, I started the process of building my case with my target date early in the fall. I worked every angle I could to be in the same places at the same time she was. I even joined the same school clubs. I also got to know her friends and used them to prime her decision by planting the seeds about going to the prom with me.

I worked for months, step-by-step, to bend the probability of a win in my favor. By the time I asked her in January, I was certain she would say *yes* (her friends told me so). With this knowledge came confidence. There was no hesitation, no debate, and no objection. My *yes* number was 100 percent.

That year my date was the prom queen. She is still the love of my life, my best friend, and my wife. That date was the most important and life-changing sale I ever closed.

Things that challenge you change you. Adversity is, and always will be, your greatest teacher.

21 | Prospecting Objections

Everybody has a plan until they get punched in the face.
                    —Mike Tyson, retired professional boxer

Following the events of 9/11, record numbers of people stepped off the tarmac and behind the wheel. It's estimated that in the aftermath of the worst attacks on American soil since Pearl Harbor, the national airlines lost up to 30 percent of their customers, causing the entire industry to teeter on the edge of collapse until the government stepped in to shore things up.

For days upon days, the 24-hour news channels blasted the horrific scenes of the planes crashing into the twin towers and the Pentagon, along with the last words of the heroes on Flight 93 before it crashed into a field in Pennsylvania.

It's no wonder that people were suddenly afraid to get on planes. They imagined the horror of being trapped on a plane hijacked by terrorists. They saw themselves in those final desperate moments making their last call to loved ones to say goodbye.

Suddenly, travel by automobile, no matter how long the trip, seemed safer. People judged, based on recent events—the ones most available in memory—that their chances of dying were far lower in their cars than on a plane.

They were wrong. 2,977 people (not including the 19 terrorists) were killed as a direct result of the terrorists turning the planes into weapons. A conservative estimate is that 1,595 additional deaths occurred due to the increase in driving and decrease in flying immediately after 9/11.[1] If you are doing the math, that is a little more than 50 percent of the total number of people killed in the attacks.

Diving deeper into the data, most of the 9/11 deaths were people on the ground. The total number of innocent people killed on the planes was just 246. Six-and-a-half times more people were killed on the roads following 9/11 than in the planes of 9/11 because people judged that driving was safer than flying.

According to the National Safety Council, you have a 1 in 114 probability of dying in a car crash versus a 1 in 9,821 chance of dying in a plane or spacecraft, including private planes.[2] In fact, there is a higher probability that you will be killed by a shark attack than a plane crash.[3] Simply put, you are far more likely to be killed driving to the airport than flying on the plane. Yet following the news of a rare plane crash, people will cancel flights in droves and get into cars.

So why did people after 9/11 falsely believe that they stood a better chance of survival in the family car than on a plane, and why should this matter to you? This strange human phenomenon is derived from the *availability bias*.[4]

Humans tend to believe that things that have just happened or are more easily recalled in memory are more likely to occur again and with greater frequency. Sadly, this makes us very, very bad at judging probability in virtually every area of life.

In a casino, for example, when a number hits and we win, our brains fool us into believing that the probability that the number will come up again is higher. Statistically speaking, the probability that the number will come up again did not change, nor did the probability that one might die in a plane crash following the terrorist attacks. That's logical, mathematical, and indisputable. However, this is not how humans calculate probability.

Human decision making and perceptions begin at the emotional level. Our brains direct our attention and perception to anomalies, catastrophes, and events that evoke emotion.

In your role as a military recruiter, you run into this bias on an almost daily basis. People assign higher probabilities of dying or other bad things happening to them in the military because of the current news cycles or information they get from their circle of influence. Then they hit you with objections.

Certainly, compared to some occupations, a career in the military carries more risk. But you have a higher likelihood of dying from a car accident (1:114), the flu (1:63), cancer and heart disease (1:7), or falling down (1:127)[5] than in the military (1:940).[6] And unlike most occupations that carry risk, the benefits and opportunities offered in the military are exceptional and are a far better match of risk to reward.

The problem is, none of this logic matters a bit when you are dealing with an illogical human being whose behavior and perceptions are being shaped by emotion. You cannot reason with emotion; instead, you must disrupt it.

This is why, when you face resistance and objections, it is critical to avoid using logic to debate your point or attempt to get your prospect to change their mind. You cannot transform emotion to logic and you cannot argue people into believing that they are wrong.

We Feel, Then We Think

In every recruiting conversation, the person who exerts the greatest amount of emotional control has the highest probability of getting the outcome they desire. Because recruiting is human, because enlisting is human, both you and your prospects are being bombarded by disruptive emotions as you interact during the recruiting process.

After an objection has been thrown on the table, in the heat of the moment, we too often treat it as a rational and logical thing. Science tells us, though, that the human decision-making process, including objections, is emotional first, then logical.

Dr. Antonio Damasio changed the way science views human decision making. He proved that emotions, not logic, guide the way we make decisions.[7] Damasio studied people whose limbic systems— the emotional center of the brain—were damaged and not working properly. Yet, these subjects had a normally functioning neocortex— the part of the brain that controls rational thought.

He discovered that people in this condition shared a peculiar commonality. It was almost impossible for them to decide. They could objectively discuss the logic and rationality of different choices, but when asked to make a decision, they found it difficult, sometimes even impossible, to choose. Without their emotions to guide them, they agonized over even the simplest choices.

Damasio's work demonstrated that emotions are central to human decision making. This is not to say that we don't make rational decisions. We certainly attempt to make decisions that we believe are in our best interest. What Damasio proved, though, is that for humans, decisions begin with emotion.

We feel, and then we think.

It is in this context that we must accept that objections are emotional. Understanding this is important, because when you try to resolve an objection with logic, without first considering its emotional origin, it's like arguing with a wall. You expend a ton of energy arguing with the wall, but the wall will not move.

Choosing a career path—especially a military career—is an emotional experience filled with stress. Prospects are overwhelmed by options, misinformation, and the endless "me-too" claims of each recruiter (military and civilian) they encounter. They are frustrated with the complicated, cluttered, and at times chaotic decision-making process. They have a cacophony of influencers chirping in their ear.

Even when prospects raise their hands and express an interest in the military, they throw out objections and resistance. They'll say they need to think about it and consider other options, fixate on what can go wrong, focus on the negatives rather than the advantages, get other people involved for their opinions, and avoid you. It's human nature.

Because objections are inherently emotional, you must first deal with objections at the emotional level before you can introduce logic. Of course, we all want those magic words that roll off our tongues like sugar and wow our prospects into complete submission. We secretly fantasize about having the perfect lines that get us past any objection. Recruiters are constantly asking:

"What do I say when they tell me . . .?"
"What should I do when they say . . .?"
"How do I respond if they ask . . .?"

In this chapter, our focus is on what to say *after* you ask for time or information and get an objection. This is when you are most likely to freeze up, argue logic, say nonsensical things, get embarrassed, and feel the sharp sting of rejection.

This inflection point is also the moment of truth when you either get past no and engage your prospect, or get your hat handed to you and walk away with nothing.

Instead of giving you generic scripts, though, we'll focus on a *Three-Step Prospecting Objection Turnaround Framework*. Frameworks make you agile. They give you a set of rails to run on that flex to changing context. The *Three-Step Prospecting Objection Turnaround Framework* is designed for both managing your disruptive emotions in the moment and pulling your prospect toward you so that it becomes easier for them to say *yes*.

To be successful in getting past *no*, you must develop poise, confidence, and emotional control. You will need to master objection turnaround frameworks to break through resistance, move past objections, and get to *yes*.

The Rule of Thirds

With prospecting interactions, your goal should be to get to a yes, no, or maybe for a conversation or interview as quickly as possible.

>   **Get to yes fast.** About one-third of the time, your prospect will say *yes* because your approach and message were spot on or because you showed up at just the right time and asked confidently. Your goal is to get these *yeses* off the table fast and avoid talking your prospect into saying no. This is where confidence matters. When you anticipate rejection, allow your fear to derail you, and come off as insecure, weak, or passive, you'll transfer those emotions to your prospect and create resistance where it didn't exist—turning a sure *yes* into a *no*.

>   **Get to no fast.** About one-third of the time the prospect will say no and mean no. Sometimes the prospect will hang up the phone on you or turn their back and walk away. Sometimes they'll be rude. Most times, the prospect will give you a direct and certain *no!* Although it sucks, a direct no is also a blessing, because it allows you to move on to the next call quickly.

>   **Get to maybe fast.** About one-third of the time the prospect will hesitate, say maybe, negotiate, or throw out an objection. This is where the rubber meets the road in recruiting—it's where you have a chance to turn a *maybe* into a *yes*.

In military recruiting, *maybe* is where you earn your stripes. The *maybes* matter because these prospects are often your best opportunities—Alphas who have many options available to them.

It's the skill and poise to deal with prospecting objections and turn them into *yeses* that gets you in front of your highest-value, most qualified prospects.

In this chapter, I'm going to give you a framework for dealing with prospecting objections that will increase your probability of turning *maybe* into *yes*. Once you master this framework, you'll gain the confidence to effectively handle anything that is thrown at you while prospecting.

The Three-Step Prospecting Objection Turnaround Framework helps you control the disruptive emotions that turn prospecting calls and interactions into painful train wrecks. Let's begin with gaining a basic understanding of the responses you get from prospects when you interrupt their day.

Prospecting RBOs

When prospecting by phone, in person, or by e-mail, direct messages, and text messaging, you'll run into three types of responses: reflex responses, brush-offs, and true objections. Collectively these are called *prospecting RBOs*.

Reflex Responses

I was traveling and realized that I'd left the cord for my iPad at home. There was an office supply store within walking distance of my hotel, so I strolled over to get one. As I entered the store, a nice young man walked up to me and asked, "May I help you?"

I responded, "I'm just looking."

As I walked away, I caught myself. I wasn't "just looking." Who the hell goes to an office supply store to "just look"? I'd gone there on purpose to get a power cord. So, I went back and asked for help, and he walked me over to the shelf where the cords were hanging.

Why did I respond this way when it clearly wasn't the truth? It was automatic, something I'd said hundreds of times. You do the same thing, too. It's a habit, a reflexive response that requires little cognitive investment.

Prospects respond to prospecting calls with reflex responses, and recruiters fall for it—treating reflex responses at face value. For the prospect it's easy. When a recruiter interrupts, hit them with a *reflex response*, then like magic, the recruiter goes away.

"I'm not interested."

"I'm already going to college."

"I have a job."

"I'm busy."

"It's not for me."

"I'm driving."

"I'm just running out the door."

"No, my daughter isn't interested in joining the military."

These are just some of the conditioned, rote responses to your interruption. The prospect is just running on autopilot.

Because prospecting objections are usually conditioned responses, the most effective way to get past them is pattern painting—disrupting the prospect's expectations for how you will respond. We'll discuss pattern painting later in the chapter.

Brush-Off

A brush-off is your prospect's nice way of telling you to bug off, avoid conflict, and let you down easy:

"Call me later."

"Get back to me in a month."

"I'm taking some time off this summer. Maybe call me in September."

"Why don't you just send over some information?" (The greatest brush-off of all time.)

Prospects have learned that recruiters, for the most part, are willing to accept these falsehoods and go away, because recruiters want to avoid conflict, too.

The brush-off doesn't feel as much like rejection. When you accept a brush-off, your brain lets you off the hook. You still have hope. You fit in, didn't cross the line, weren't too pushy. You avoided being rejected—being kicked out of the cave.

Except that for recruiters, getting snowed by a brush-off is like pushing a rope. You delude yourself into believing that you've accomplished something:

"He must be interested because he said to call him back in a month or two."

"She wants more information, so she must be interested."

But you get nowhere. A brush-off is just a falsehood that both parties are conditioned to believe to circumvent the pain of conflict and rejection.

True Objections

True objections on prospecting calls tend to be more transparent and logical rebuttals to your request. They typically come with a reason:

"There is really no reason for us to meet right now because I was just accepted to college."

"I'm leaving for a family vacation and can't talk right now."

"I spoke to the Air Force, and they said I wasn't qualified."

"I'd love to talk, but I'm going to move to Arizona to live with my brother and work for his company."

"My parents won't let me join the military."

"I'm already talking to the Marine Corps."

When you get true objections, you must use your good judgment. There are three decisions paths:

1. Turn the objection around and meet anyway.
2. Shift gears and gather information—or flip the call into a referral.
3. Hang up, move on, and come back to the prospect at a better time or never.

Prospecting RBOs Can Be Anticipated in Advance

At every Fanatical Military Recruiting Boot Camp, I ask a simple question of the participants: "How many ways can a prospect tell you *no* on a prospecting call?"

The most common answer (accompanied by the obligatory eye roll): *It's infinite.*

Sadly, this is how most recruiters think. They approach each prospecting objection as a unique, random event and thus wing it on every call. This is a big mistake—in recruiting, winging it is always stupid and at no time more so than when prospecting. It is almost impossible to control the emotional and neurochemical responses to rejection in the harsh environment of prospecting without a plan.

The truth is, prospecting RBOs are not unique. There are a finite number of ways a prospect will tell you *no*. Better yet, there are a common set of RBOs faced by military recruiters, and usually just three to five of these make up 80 percent or more of prospecting objections. In general, most RBOs come in the form of:

- Not interested
- Don't know what I'm going to do
- Not qualified
- Parents won't let me join
- Too dangerous
- Don't want to leave home
- Don't like the current Commander in Chief
- Already talking to another branch
- Already have a job
- Want to take some time off first
- Going to college
- The military is not for me
- I need to speak to someone else before . . .
- Too busy
- Just send information
- Overwhelmed—too many things going on
- Family obligations
- Don't want to go to boot camp
- Just looking/checking you out (inbound leads)

Prospects don't always use these exact words. For example, instead of saying, "I'm too busy" they may say, "I've got football practice and a test I need to study for." The words are different, but the intent is the same—I'm busy.

When I ask participants in our Fanatical Military Recruiting courses to list all the possible RBOs they can think of, we rarely get past 15. When I ask them to list the ones they hear most often, it's rarely more than five.

Making a list of the most common RBOs you encounter during prospecting interactions is the first step toward learning to anticipate RBOs and crafting effective responses. Take a moment right now and use Table 21.1 to list all the prospecting RBOs you run into. Then rank them from most frequent to least frequent.

Table 21.1 Listing RBOs

Common RBOs	Rank Based on Frequency

Planning for Prospecting RBOs

You are going to get prospecting objections, and they will trigger your disruptive emotions. But since virtually every RBO you get on a prospecting call can be anticipated, you may plan responses in advance, gain control of your emotions, disrupt your prospects' patterns, and flip the script.

To master and become effective at turning around prospecting RBOs, you simply need to:

1. Identify all the potential RBOs (see the previous exercise).
2. Leverage the Three-Step Prospecting Objection Turnaround Framework to develop simple, repeatable *scripts* that you say without having to think—thus allowing you to rise above your emotions.

Why have a repeatable practiced script for RBOs? We've explored the emotional response to anticipated, perceived, or real rejection. The fight-or-flight response kicks in, blood rushes from your neocortex (rational brain), and you can't think. This makes it very difficult to construct messages that address the RBO in the moment, during lightning-fast prospecting exchanges.

In emotionally tense situations, scripts free your mind, releasing you from the burden of worrying about what to say and putting you in complete control of the situation. A practiced script makes your voice intonation, speaking style, and flow sound confident, relaxed, authentic, and professional—even when your emotions are raging beneath the surface.

Scripts work especially well with prospecting RBOs because you tend to get the same ones again and again. To observe the power of scripts, just go see a movie. Every TV show, movie, and play is scripted. Were they not, they wouldn't be entertaining.

Notice the difference when a politician is speaking off script in a confrontation with reporters as opposed to giving a speech with the aid of a teleprompter. On stage, the politician is incredibly convincing. But without a script, he stumbles on his words and makes many of the same mistakes recruiters make when winging it with RBOs on prospecting calls.

The worry for most recruiters, though, is "I won't sound like myself when I use a script." The concern about sounding canned is legitimate. In recruiting, authenticity matters. This is exactly why actors, politicians, and top recruiters rehearse and practice. They work and work until the script sounds natural and becomes their voice.

Scripts are a powerful way to control your emotions and manage your message, but they must be internalized. Developing your RBO turnaround scripts requires effort. You must tailor your messages to your unique situation. You must practice, test your assumptions, and *iterate* until you hone messages that work and sound authentic.

The good news is that you already have the habit of saying certain things certain ways on prospecting calls. So begin with analyzing what you are already doing. Then formalize what is working into a script that can be repeated with success, time and again.

Take a moment now to write down in Table 21.2 your five most frequent prospecting RBOs and how you currently respond

Table 21.2   Analyzing RBOs and Your Responses

Top Five Prospecting RBOs	How You Respond Now

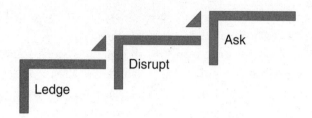

Figure 21.1   Three-Step Prospecting Objection Turnaround Framework

to them. Consider what is working and what is not working. Look for patterns in your messages. Think about the messages that make you feel and sound the most authentic.

The Three-Step Prospecting Objection Turnaround Framework

For reflex responses, brush-offs, and objections during prospecting, you'll deploy a simple but powerful three-step framework (see Figure 21.1):

1. Ledge
2. Disrupt
3. Ask

You learned earlier in the chapter that a framework is like a set of rails. It acts as a guide to give you structure but doesn't lock you into a one-size-fits-all process. Frameworks give you agility and authenticity in the heat of the moment, allowing you to shift your message to the unique situation of each prospect.

The Ledge

We've established that the initial physiological fight-or-flight response is involuntary. The adrenaline rushing through your bloodstream is released without your consent. In this state, with your body and brain drunk on neurochemicals, it is very difficult to retain your emotional composure.

But the effect of adrenaline is short-lived. The fight-or-flight response is only meant to get you out of trouble long enough to allow you to consider your options rationally and make the next move. The secret to gaining control of disruptive emotions in the moment is simply giving your rational brain (neocortex) a chance to catch up and take executive control.

In her book *Emotional Alchemy*, Tara Bennett-Goleman calls this the "magic quarter second"[8] that allows you to keep the disruptive emotions you feel from becoming emotional reactions you express.

In fast-moving situations—like prospecting objections—to deal with disruptive emotions effectively, you need to quickly regain your poise and control of the conversation. Because prospecting objections tend to evoke strong emotional responses, the *ledge* gives you the magic quarter second you need to rise above your emotions and choose your response.

The ledge can be a statement, acknowledgment, agreement, or question. It is a simple but powerful technique for gaining control of your disruptive emotions when you feel fight or flight kicking in. Examples include:

"It sounds like you've been through this before."

"That's exactly why I called."

"I figured you might say that."

"A lot of people feel the same way."

"I get why you might feel that way."

"That makes sense."

"That's interesting—can you tell me why this is important to you?"

"How so?"

"Would you help me understand?

194 Fanatical Military Recruiting

"Interesting—could you walk me through your concern?"

"Just to be sure I understand your question, could you elaborate a little more?"

The ledge technique works because it's a memorized, automatic response that does not require you to think. This is important because as soon as our old friend fight or flight takes over, cognitive capacity deteriorates.[9]

Instead of stumbling through a nonsensical answer that makes you come off as defensive, weak, or unknowledgeable, or damaging the relationship with an argument, you simply use the ledge technique that you have prepared in advance.

Disrupt

Traditionally, trainers have taught recruiters to "overcome objections." I often hear trainers use the phrase "combatting objections." Some teach "rebuttals." Sadly, this poor advice derails recruiters in their quest to get past *no*.

It's also common to hear leaders tell recruiters to "never take 'no' for an answer." The intention is to encourage persistence. I get it and understand the intent. In recruiting, persistence and resilience are critical mind-sets. Especially with prospecting and top-of-the-funnel activities, not letting *no* stop you is an asset.

But some recruiters mistake "never take 'no' for an answer" with "argue your prospect into submission." This is one of the many reasons, including the disruptive emotions of attachment and desperation, that recruiters attempt to argue or pitch prospects into changing their minds. Objections become debates that must be won. Prospects and their parents are viewed as adversaries who must be conquered. *No* becomes a competition.

Overcoming doesn't work. It has never really worked. The more you push, the more they'll dig their heels in and resist you. This behavior is called *psychological reactance*.

People predictably rebel in the face of a debate or when choices are taken away from them. When someone tells you that you're wrong, your response is quick and emotional (even when you really *are* wrong): "Oh yeah? I'll show you!"

Psychological reactance unleashes your inner brat. This is the reason you cannot argue other people into believing they are wrong. No matter the logic of your argument, data, or supporting facts, the people you are arguing with will dig their heels in and argue back. When you trigger reactance, you push your prospects away from you rather than pulling them toward you. For this reason, overcoming, combatting, rebutting, and debating do not work.

The attempt to overcome creates animosity, exasperation, and frustration for both the prospects, who get bulldozed with an argument about why they are wrong, and the recruiter, who creates even more resistance and harsher rejection with this approach. So, prospects obfuscate, put up smoke screens, become stubborn and illogical, and even lie.

There is a better way. Rather than viewing prospects as adversaries, rather than attempting to prevail in an argument, leverage the way the brain works to paint patterns, disrupt your prospect's expectations, turn them around, and pull them in.

Pattern Painting

Much like a computer, our brains can process only so much information at one time. As the cognitive load[10] grows, the brain slows down and becomes less efficient. It is unable to focus, and attention control diminishes.

From a purely evolutionary sense, this inability to focus can put you in danger. Should there be a threat nearby—say a saber-toothed tiger crouched in the weeds, a bus rolling down the street, or a shooter on a rooftop—and you are so overwhelmed with incoming sensory information that you fail to see it, then *bam!* You're dead.

Moving slowly tended to remove a person's DNA from the gene pool, so human brains evolved to think fast. With so much sensory information hitting us at one time, we needed a way to focus on only those environmental anomalies that might be dangers or opportunities.

The human brain became a pattern monster, ignoring most incoming data so it could focus on things that stuck out—different, new, dangerous. Your brain is a master at grabbing the billions of bits of information in the environment around you, interpreting the patterns in them, and behaving appropriately (in most cases) in response to those patterns.[11]

If your brain did not leverage patterns for decision making and adaptive response to the world around you, you'd become overwhelmed and be unable to function. Disrupting patterns begins with understanding two facts about the human brain.

1. **It is tasked with keeping you alive** and therefore focuses on things in the environment that are unexpected and could pose a threat, while ignoring things that are the same (patterns) to ensure that it does not miss the former.
2. **It is lazy,** preferring the path of least resistance or cognitive load when making decisions. When the brain sees a pattern that is similar to other patterns, instead of taking the time to analyze whether the two things are different in any way, it assumes they are the same and uses that shortcut to make a quick decision.

If suddenly there was a loud noise nearby, your attention would be torn from these words and pulled toward that sound. Your brain would begin scanning your surroundings for anything out of place that could be a threat while also preparing you to deal with that threat. This is your fight-or-flight response. For the moment, a part of your brain called the amygdala has taken control of your emotions and behavior.

Think of the brain as a nesting Russian doll.

- The big doll on the outside is the neocortex. This is your gray matter—your rational brain.
- The middle doll is the limbic system—your emotional brain.

- The smallest doll is your cerebellum or autonomic brain—it manages all the little (but still important) things like breathing, so you can concentrate on thinking.

All three brains are connected by the amygdala, a small structure within the brain that is housed in the limbic system.

The amygdala is the hub that processes all sensory input, connecting the rational, emotional, and autonomic parts of your brain. It is the center for emotions, emotional behavior, and motivation. Fear and pleasure are the language of the amygdala, and it exerts a massive and compulsory influence over your emotional behavior.

To avoid wasting precious resources on things that don't matter, the amygdala focuses on and responds to environmental disruptions—anything different, unexpected, or new that it deems important to your survival, both physically and socially. The simple cognitive shortcut of ignoring boring patterns and being alert to anything that disrupts patterns is a key reason for our success as a species.

Your prospect has an expectation for how you will respond when they tell you no. They have an expectation for what you will most likely do next. When your behaviors match their expectations, no thinking is required; they just react.

When you disrupt expectations, though, it pulls prospects toward you. Different is sexy. Different sells. The amygdala loves bright, shiny things. *Pattern painting*—grabbing attention—is at the heart of the objection turnaround framework. Doing the unexpected is how you flip your prospect's reflex script, turn them around, and pull them toward you.

Some examples of disrupt statements

When they say they're already going to college, instead of arguing that you can help them with money if they just give you a chance, respond with something that is completely unexpected:

"Awesome. Sounds like you really have it together. All I want is a few minutes of your time to learn more about you and provide some additional information on our college tuition benefits. At a minimum, you'll have the peace of mind that you've fully explored all of your options."

When they say they're busy, instead of arguing them into how you will only take a little bit of their time, disrupt their pattern by agreeing with them:

"That's exactly why I called; I figured you would be. All I want to do is find a time that's more convenient for you."

When they say, "Just send me some information," you can call their bluff and force engagement, or bring another RBO to the surface with:

"That's fantastic! I'm happy to hear that you are interested in learning more. But we have so much information available and the last thing I want to do is overwhelm you. Can you tell me specifically what information you'd like to see?"

If they identify information they'd like to see, respond with:

"That's exactly why we should get together. Once I learn more about your situation, I'll tailor an information package just for you."

When they say, "I'm not interested," respond with:

"That makes sense. Most people aren't interested the first time I call, and that's exactly why we should meet."

It is also important to avoid using words that only recruiters use. As soon as you do, you play right into expectations, become a pattern, and trigger another reflex response. Overused phrases like "Reaching out," "I just wanted to," "That's great," and "I understand" turn you into an easy-to-ignore pattern.

Ask

Back to the most important discipline in recruiting. To get what you want, you must *ask* for what you want. You may deliver the perfect objection turnaround, but if you don't *ask* again, you won't get the outcome you desire.

The *ask step* is where most prospecting objection turnarounds fall apart. The recruiter hesitates and waits for the prospect to do the work. They don't, and they won't.

You must control your emotions and ask again for what you want, assumptively and assertively, without hesitation, directly following your turnaround script. When you ask, about half of the time they'll throw out another RBO—one that tends to be closer to the truth. Be prepared to turn it around and ask again.

What you should never do, though, is fight. It isn't worth it. When you get two RBOs and still can't turn your prospect around, graciously move on and come back to them another day. As they say, there are plenty of fish in the sea.

Putting It All Together

It is essential that you avoid overcomplicating this process. You need turnaround scripts that work for you and sound natural coming from your lips. They need to make you sound authentic, real, and confident.

Keep them simple so that they are easy for you to remember and repeat. They don't need to be perfect, and they won't work every time, but you need scripts that give you the highest probability of getting a *yes*.

Table 21.3   Build a Turnaround Script

Common Prospecting RBOs	Ledge	Disrupt

Now it's time to build your own scripts. Using Table 21.3, start with your five most common RBOs and consider your unique situation. Write down a ledge and construct a disrupt statement.

Once you complete the first pass, walk away from it for a day, and then come back and do it again. You'll find that this process gives your brain a chance to adjust to the messaging process and will help you revise your scripts and make them better.

PART VIII

Face-to-Face and Digital Prospecting

22 | Face-to-Face Prospecting

Nothing replaces being in the same room, face-to-face.
—Peter Guber, executive and entrepreneur

While the telephone is fast and efficient, face-to-face prospecting (F2F) is slow and inefficient. Done incorrectly and randomly, you can easily burn an entire day, engage few prospects, and accomplish little more than wasting the government's fuel. For scores of recruiters, face-to-face prospecting is their only prospecting channel, and the primary reason they are not making mission.

Yet face-to-face prospecting is highly effective because when you get face to face it's easier to qualify, build relationships, and convert conversations into interviews. This is why you should plan it in advance and be intentional.

Face-to-face prospecting is the foundation of a balanced prospecting methodology in military recruiting. It will and should consume the majority of the time you block for prospecting.

Balance is the key. When you leverage F2F within a balanced prospecting routine that includes all prospecting channels, you'll maximize your recruiting day and squeeze every drop of opportunity from it.

There are three core objectives of face-to-face prospecting:

- **Qualifying:** In many cases, people will give you more information in person than they will over the phone. Plus, you gain insight on your prospects' motivations, urgency, and influencers.
- **Setting up interviews and next steps:** If your prospect is motivated and qualified, don't wait—set up an appointment for an interview or test on the spot. You may also want to invite prospects who are not quite ready for an interview to take practice tests or meet you at upcoming events.
- **Building familiarity and nurturing relationships:** By putting a face with a name and building relationships, you open the door to future conversations when the time is right.

The Four-Step Face-to-Face Prospecting Framework

The primary objectives of face-to-face prospecting are similar to that of telephone prospecting—set up interviews and gather qualifying information.

But where telephone prospecting is about what you *say*, prospecting in-person is about what you *ask*. It's about engaging prospects in conversations. With face-to-face prospecting, building familiarity and relationships takes center stage—especially when working your schools.

The Four-Step Face-to-Face Prospecting Framework is similar to the telephone prospecting framework. The main difference between the face-to-face framework and the phone process is that

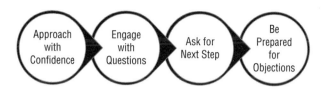

Figure 22.1 Four-Step Face-to-Face Prospecting Framework

the IPP will move along at a slower pace, and there will typically be more dialogue. Figure 22.1 shows the framework.

1. **Approach with confidence and expect a positive outcome.** Emotions are contagious, and when you are meeting face to face, there is no substitute for enthusiasm and relaxed confidence. These are the emotions that attract and pull prospects toward you. You must approach face-to-face prospecting conversations with absolute confidence.

   Be bold—even if you have to fake it. At events, step out from behind the table. Keep your hands out of your pockets. Smile and invite people in. Listen rather than pitch. Be conversational while you gather qualifying information. Don't beat around the bush and don't hesitate. You are a noncommissioned officer in the United States military. You've earned the right to be there and be respected. You are a professional.

2. **Engage with open-ended questions.** Engage in a conversation rather than an interrogation. Eighty percent of human communication is visual. Face-to-face prospecting is powerful because unlike most other prospecting channels, you use all of your senses to communicate. You'll be most effective when you relax, are yourself, ask open-ended questions that encourage others to talk, listen, and engage in meaningful conversations.

   Avoid the temptation to pitch. As soon as you start pitching, your ears turn off, and so does your prospect. It's all about asking the prospect the right questions and demonstrating that you care. You must focus your attention on them and their situation.

Consider what it feels like to be on the other end of a conversation where someone is just talking about themselves. It's boring. As soon as you start pitching, your prospect can tell that you care about nothing other than getting what you want, and that is why they zone out, make you feel uncomfortable, and put up emotional walls.

However, when you get them talking about themselves, show interest, give them your complete attention, and listen, they will engage, be more transparent, and look for ways to help you. Make the conscious decision to focus your attention on your prospect. Tell yourself to listen instead of pitching. Make a commitment to slow down and ask questions, really listen to the answers, and ask relevant follow-up questions.

3. **Ask for the next step.** If you don't ask, you won't get. When meeting prospects in person, be prepared to ask confidently for a face-to-face interview, an appointment to take the test, a practice test, a chance to meet their parents, an invitation to come to an upcoming event, etc.

4. **Be prepared for objections.** When you ask for next steps, you're going to get objections. Develop and prepare turnarounds in advance. Review the previous chapter on turning around prospecting objections for techniques that will help you get past *no*.

First Impressions: Making an Emotional Connection

"Why did you join the Marines?" I was sitting next to Lance Corporal Ralls on a flight from Atlanta to San Diego.

Ralls smiled. "It just felt right?"

"How do you mean?"

"Well, I'd first considered enlisting in the Army. My dad was a career soldier who retired as a First Sergeant, and my older brother is a Ranger. But I don't know. There was just something about the Army recruiter I didn't like. I honestly can't put my finger on it.

"But Sergeant Williams, my recruiter, he was different. I met him at a school event and we instantly hit it off. He was so confident and relaxed. I liked how professional he always looked—his entire demeanor. He always had great things to say about the Marine Corps. It made me want to be a Marine like him, and I've never looked back."

Like Lance Corporal Ralls, we all make judgments when we first meet people. These judgments, which are both imperfect and emotional, have a lasting impact on how we view and interact with others. In Lance Corporal Ralls's case, first impressions caused him to choose the Marines over the Army.

People make these same imperfect judgments about you. First impressions are about likability, and likability is the gateway to building emotional connections with prospects, parents, and community partners. When people like you, the probability increases that they will be open to answering your questions and engaging in conversations.

Triggering the Negativity and Safety Biases

Despite the almost universal perception that military recruiters will say and do anything to get an enlistment, I rarely meet recruiters who lack basic integrity. Most recruiters:

- Want the best for their prospects and applicants
- Do the right thing
- Keep their promises
- Tell the truth
- Believe in the career path they are offering

The trap recruiters fall into, though, is the false belief that good intentions are enough. Prospects are not judging your trustworthiness based on *your* intentions. Instead, they judge you based on *their* intentions.

Your qualified prospects are at a pivotal point in their lives. They are young and have an abundance of options. They also have a circle of influencers (COI)—parents, peers, extended family, teachers, coaches, and mentors—around them, all with opinions about what path in life they should choose.

Making poor choices about career and educational paths carries real risk for your prospects. In our hypercompetitive global marketplace, dominated by disruptive change, the penalties for making mistakes can be severe. This, by the way, is why making no change—sticking with the status quo—is often the emotionally safe choice, even when staying put is illogical or dysfunctional.

Fear, insecurity, lack of trust, misunderstanding, dislike, and uncertainty are the genesis of resistance and objections.

Prospects and their parents are scrutinizing you and the military. They are looking for congruence in your words, nonverbal communication, and actions. You are on stage and everything about you is being observed. What you must not forget is that humans focus attention on things that stick out, and anything negative sticks out like a sore thumb.

This is the *negativity bias*. The human brain is attuned to what's wrong about someone rather than what is right. Negative things have a greater impact on behavior than positive things. Negative messages, thoughts, and images grab and hold our attention. Over time, negative perceptions add up, building the case that you cannot be trusted.

You trigger the negativity bias when you pitch instead of allowing your prospect and their parents talk. In these moments of insecurity, you overwhelm the prospect with tedious details about the recruiting and enlistment process, begin dump-trucking features and benefits of military service, start talking about yourself, or bring up negative aspects of military service. You:

- Answer unasked questions.
- Bring up perceived objections, even though the prospect hasn't mentioned the issue.

- Project your own issues onto your prospect.
- Introduce potentially negative issues about the military to "get them on the table."
- Talk about potentially negative aspects of a military career out of context.

Humans live with an underlying fear that change will make things worse. We are driven to avoid making irreversible decisions. When faced with options, we gravitate to the one that is perceived to carry the least risk.

In his book *Thinking, Fast and Slow*, Daniel Kahneman, the father of cognitive bias research, writes:

> Organisms that placed more urgency on avoiding threats than they did maximizing opportunities were more likely to pass on their genes. So, over time, the prospect of losses has become a more powerful motivator on your behavior than the promise of gains.[1]

This *safety bias* causes your prospect's brain to be more aware of bad things (what could go wrong) than good things (what could go right). In evolutionary terms it makes sense. Although you might miss the opportunity for a good thing, such as a free lunch, if you were not paying attention to risk in your environment, you could end up *being* lunch—a very bad thing.

As humans, we tend to be attracted to safe choices and safe environments. The military, as a rule, is not perceived as safe—especially during rough news cycles. As a military recruiter, you pose a threat—especially to parents who are hardwired to protect their children from harm at all costs.

Your prospects are worried. "What if things go wrong?" They worry that you won't live up to your promises. They worry that you'll manipulate them.

And why shouldn't they? They've heard the saying: *"How do you know when a recruiter is lying? When their mouth is moving."*

Prospects and parents carry this emotional baggage with them into conversations with you. And because humans remember negative events far more vividly than positive ones, prospects believe that past negative events (such as war, accidents, or negative stories from people in their circle of influence about the military) will be more likely to happen in the future.

The safety bias creates a formidable emotional wall. The number-one reason why prospects choose not to move forward with you to the next step is the fear of negative future consequences.

These pernicious cognitive biases, working in concert, cause your prospects' and their parents' subconscious minds to magnify every flaw, every risk, and every concern about you and the military. They feel uncertain, unsure, and afraid. For recruiters, despite all their concerns about the competition in this War for Talent, the negativity and safety biases will always be their most formidable adversaries.

The Five Questions That Matter Most in Recruiting

In every recruiting conversation and throughout the recruiting process, prospects are mentally asking five questions about you:

1. Do I like you?
2. Do you listen to me?
3. Do you make me feel important?
4. Do you get me and my problems?
5. Do I trust and believe you?

These are the five most important questions in recruiting. Ultra-high performers get this. From the first moment they engage a prospect until the new Soldier, Sailor, Airman, or Marine ships, they are intensely focused on answering these five questions with a *yes!*

The five questions are being asked and answered by both prospects and parents at the conscious and subconscious levels. The questions originate from emotion and are answered with emotion.

How you answer these questions for each prospect will determine the outcome of your recruiting conversations—positive or negative—and increase or decrease your probability of a win. When you answer the five questions in the affirmative, it becomes almost impossible for qualified prospects not to enlist with you.

It is the first question—"Do I like you?"—that's so critical to your success with neutralizing the negativity and safety biases. It's important that you never forget that people enlist with *you* first and then your branch of the military. Though not every qualified prospect who likes you will enlist, you can be sure that those who don't like you will not.

Unlike trust, being perceived as likable or unlikable occurs in mere moments and begins in your prospect's subconscious—long before they are aware of how they feel about you at the conscious level. The Army recruiter who turned Lance Corporal Ralls off is the poster child for the saying, "You never get a second chance to make a great first impression."

The word *likable* is defined by the Merriam-Webster dictionary as "having qualities that bring about a favorable regard." We all, to some extent, have qualities and characteristics that make us naturally likable to certain types of people and personalities, though at the same time we possess qualities that make us naturally unlikable to others (see the next chapter on flexing your style).

The problem we face in recruiting is we don't always get to choose those with whom we interact. Many of the people we encounter will not be naturally attracted to us. Complicating things more are the pre-judgments that all people bring into relationships. These perceptions, which include but are not limited to cultural, racial, and socioeconomic biases, are also beyond our control.

There was just "something" about the Army recruiter that Ralls didn't like. There are myriad reasons a prospect may not like you, and it's true that many of the reasons are completely outside of your control. Therefore, when you meet new prospects, it's critical that you control those aspects of likability that are within your power to control.

Likability: The Gateway to Emotional Connections

Sergeant Lentz leaned through the window of the Suburban. His eyes darted away as he admitted the truth. He was under heavy pressure because he'd missed his recruiting mission two months in a row, and as he neared the end of the quarter, it looked certain that he was going to roll another zero month.

Desperate for help, he'd flagged me down after training. He explained that he'd left his last 11 recruiting meetings without getting a commitment for a next step. "I just don't understand it," he said, almost pleading. "I tell them all about the National Guard and why they should join, and then nothing. They say, 'Thanks for the information,' and the conversation is over."

"Sergeant Lentz," I asked, "when you think back on those meetings, who is doing most of the talking—you or the prospect?"

He took a step back and looked down at his boots. "I guess I am," he replied softly.

Lentz, like so many recruiters, has a problem—a problem that is easily fixable but nonetheless a problem. When the prospects and parents to whom he's selling the National Guard ask the question "Do I like you?" about Sergeant Lentz, the answer is "no."

Now don't get me wrong. Sergeant Lentz is a very likable man. He's polite, nice, and funny, and he cares deeply about mission to recruit the brightest and most talented young men and women into the National Guard. What makes him unlikable is *his approach.*

When prospecting face-to-face, your goal is to win other people over by making them feel that they are the center of your attention—to make them feel significant or important.

Your objective is to initiate and then, over time, nurture a deep emotional connection.

Emotional connections are crucial to influencing the decisions and behaviors of prospects and their influencers. The gateway to emotional connections is likability.

Of course, we know that likability alone is not a guarantee of an enlistment. It takes more. *People enlist with recruiters they like, trust, and believe will help them build a better future.* Thus, proper execution of the recruiting process is critical to positive recruiting outcomes.

Likability comes first, though. If you are not likable, you have no chance. Prospects don't engage with recruiters they don't like.

Now think for a moment about what makes another person likable. Likable people are nice, polite, respectful, courteous, thoughtful, and confident; they have a positive disposition, have an appealing outward appearance, a smile, upbeat tone of voice, and they listen. They demonstrate that they like you by giving you their sincere attention and listening. We tend to like people who like us.

Now, think about most recruiters. Most recruiters are nice, polite, respectful, and relatively confident; they are positive, look good, smile, and sound great on the phone. In general, most recruiters easily pull off these likable behaviors except for one.

They talk instead of listen.

Pitch Slapping

Nobody likes a pitch. Not you, not me, not your prospects. Look at it this way. If you could choose to hang out with people who spent the entire time you were together talking about themselves or a person who invested the time listening to you, which would you choose? For most people, that choice is easy and obvious.

The struggle Sergeant Lentz was facing is a problem shared by thousands of recruiters. They show up, throw up, and are flabbergasted that their prospects don't respond with open arms.

Instead of building emotional connections, they pitch slap prospects and turn them off.

In your initial interactions during face-to-face prospecting, prospects keep their emotional wall up and you at arm's length. To bend the win probability in your favor, you'll need to lower the wall.

Yet when your prospect is hesitant to engage, the situation becomes uncomfortable and awkward. You attempt to ask open-ended questions but only get terse answers.

In this emotionally uncomfortable situation, average recruiters succumb to disruptive emotions and impatiently shift from questions to pitching, effectively killing engagement and discovery. It's not that these recruiters are clueless. They know what to do. They're just so overwhelmed by emotions that they don't do it. These emotions include:

- **Fear of the unknown:** Since the recruiter doesn't know what the prospect might say, they dominate the conversation to feel safe.
- **Actualization:** When the prospect's emotional wall is up and they are not leaning in and engaging, the recruiter doesn't feel validated. In this moment of insecurity, the recruiter begins talking as a way to protect themselves from potential rejection.
- **Attachment to control:** Recruiters falsely believe that to be in control they must be doing the talking.
- **Lack of comfort with silence:** Whenever there is silence, the recruiter becomes uncomfortable and fills the void with words.
- **Impatience:** The recruiter gets frustrated with the prospect's short answers or slow pace and takes over the conversation.
- **Need for significance:** The recruiter doesn't feel appreciated when the prospect is talking, so they interrupt to prove how smart they are.

Meanwhile, within this arc of disruptive emotions, the prospect's negativity bias is kicking in. Their subconscious mind is homing in on and magnifying the things about the recruiter that they don't like. They don't know why, but there is something about the recruiter that "they just don't like."

At the conscious level, prospects find it excruciating when a recruiter is droning on and on about their own story or the benefits of enlisting in the military. People don't enlist with recruiters they don't like, and they don't like recruiters who pitch slap them.

Ultra-high performers feel these same disruptive emotions. We all do. The difference is that they are aware of how destructive the behaviors spawned by these emotions are to human-to-human relationships. Even when the prospect prompts them with a battery of questions, UHPs resist the open invitation to pitch and instead ask questions to get the other person talking.

Keys to Being More Likable

As a military recruiter, you are always on stage. When you walk into a room in uniform, you instantly grab everyone's attention. But, answering your prospect's question "Do I like you?" is way deeper, more complex, and far more important than most recruiters consider. Being likable requires effort, strategy, and intentional focus. To be more likable, adopt these habits:

Smile. A pleasant, sincere smile is the best way to make a great first impression. Humans are naturally attracted to other humans who are smiling. So be aware of your facial expression and put a smile on your face.

Speak in a pleasant tone. Like smiling, your voice tone and inflection can cause a prospect to instantly like or dislike you. Your voice should be as neutral and free of regional dialects as possible, friendly, and upbeat. Put a smile on your face and it will shine through your voice.

Be polite. You already know this because it has been drilled into you. People who are rude, impolite, and discourteous are unlikable. Unless you were raised in a barn by animals, someone taught you basic manners. Put those manners to work in all interactions with prospects and their parents. They will notice.

Pay attention to your body language. Your body language can send the message that you are confident and approachable or that you are insecure, unapproachable, and unlikable.

Focus your attention. In today's demanding work environment, it is easy to become distracted. Wherever you are, be there. This is essential when it comes to first impressions. You must develop the self-discipline to shut everything else out and remain completely focused on your prospect.

Adapt your communication style. People tend to be attracted to and more trusting of people who are like themselves (similarity bias). Therefore, when you flex your preferred or dominant communication style to complement that of the other person, you become more similar and therefore more likable.

Be enthusiastic. Enthusiasm (passion) sells. Enthusiasm is transferable and infectious. Your enthusiasm is driven by your attitude and beliefs, so it is critical to work consistently to build and retain a winning attitude. One note, though: Few things are more off-putting than insincere enthusiasm, so be careful not to get carried away.

Be confident. Weak people repel. Arrogant people are turn-offs. Confident people attract. Confidence is a reflection of your self-image, attitude, knowledge, uniform, the words you choose, and body language.

Put Your Recruiting Goggles On

Staff Sergeant Monroe pulled the car to the curb, rolled down the window, and motioned to the two young men on the sidewalk. As they walked over, he asked, "What are you guys up to this summer?"

Thirty minutes later we were walking across a park where a pickup basketball game was in progress. We had conversations with half a dozen young men and got phone numbers from a couple of the ones who were interested.

Later that afternoon we stopped at a convenience store to get soda, spent 15 minutes in a conversation with the young lady behind the counter, and scheduled an interview with her.

Poor-performing recruiters are often so oblivious that they are blind to the prospects that are standing right next to them. Ultra-high performers like Monroe always have their "recruiting goggles" on. They train themselves to be acutely aware of all opportunities to engage the people around them. They are always on—fanatical. Looking around every corner, behind every bush, and on every street corner for their next prospect.

Prospects are everywhere—on the street, working in retail and restaurants, on construction sites, at the gym. When you see potential prospects, put your recruiting foot on the recruiting brake, get out of your recruiting car, and engage them. Ask engaging questions and get them talking. Maybe they are eligible, or maybe they know someone else you should be talking to.

Remain alert and be aware of what is happening around you. But let's be clear. Awareness without action is useless. Be fanatical. Carry a pocket full of business cards with you wherever you go. Walk up to people, ask questions, and hand them your business card. Sure, some people might get irritated, but most people will help you, talk to you, and give you a chance.

Put your recruiting goggles on.

23 | Text Messaging

Sometimes I text the "wrong" person . . . on purpose. Just to start a conversation.
—Frank Warren, boxing manager and promoter

There is absolutely no doubt that text messaging is a powerful prospecting and communication tool in modern military recruiting. It's fast and easy, and it's the preferred communication tool for many of the prospects you engage. It's not uncommon to make an outbound prospecting call on the telephone and have the prospect text you back with a question about who you are and what you want.

Text messaging is part of a balanced prospecting methodology. But there are some important rules. Rule one is that it must be used judiciously. Blasting text messages out indiscriminately can turn prospects off and hurt your personal brand. It can also get your number blocked—which means you lose both the text and phone channel for reaching the prospect.

People are averse to getting random text messages from people they don't know—especially recruiters.

The people we text with are most often people we know. Text has become the go-to medium for communication with family and friends. People, including you and me, don't want their text message in-boxes invaded by strangers. This is because it *feels* extremely personal.

Since texting is so personal, it can be a powerful channel for getting the attention of prospects. Because it so personal, though, your text messages can easily be interpreted as intrusions or violations of your prospect's privacy. For this reason, timing and technique are more important than with any other prospecting channel.

What makes text messaging such a valuable prospecting channel is the total integration of mobile phones into the lives of your prospects. Your prospects might lose their keys or wallet, but they will never lose their phones. Their phones are with them 24/7. Your prospects sleep with them and eat with them. Your prospecting calls, e-mails, social in-box messages, and text messages all go through this single ubiquitous device.

Familiarity Is Everything with Text

We talk to strangers on the phone, e-mail strangers, and meet strangers in person, but we rarely text strangers. This is why, more than with any other prospecting channel, familiarity is critical for prospecting via text. The probability that your text message will convert—compel your prospect to take action—increases exponentially if your text comes after contact through another channel.

For example, when you are prospecting by phone, if you call a prospect multiple times—meaning that your prospect sees your number pop up on their screen on several occasions—the probability that they text you back goes up versus calling only once. When you meet a student at an event, talk to them in the hall, engage in a phone conversation, connect on social media, or meet them out in the community, texting becomes an appropriate channel.

This is not to say that you shouldn't take a gamble on a text message to a hard-to-reach prospect when all other means have been exhausted. When you have nothing to lose, the chance of causing offense is worth the risk.

One key reason why text messages work is that most people feel compelled to read and/or respond to them immediately. This is why familiarity plays an important role in getting prospects to respond to your text messages (and not report you as spam or block your number completely).

Text messaging works best as an integrated part of a larger prospecting system and as part of a strategy rather than a standalone channel. According to a recent study,[1] a text message sent alone converts at 4.8 percent. That same message, if sent after a phone contact, increases conversion by 112.6 percent.

You can amplify that impact even further when your text message follows an e-mail contact or social media interaction. And you gain even more traction when your text follows a positive face-to-face interaction. The better the prospect knows you, the more effective your prospecting text message will be.

Use Text to Anchor Face-to-Face Conversations

Text messages are excellent vehicles for setting appointments following face-to-face interactions at school and community events and other situations where you've had a positive face-to-face encounter with a prospect. Many of these encounters end with a vague promise to get together sometime in the future. Yet most of those promises are never fulfilled because you get busy and fail to follow up, or your prospect gets busy and ignores your e-mails and phone calls.

Text messaging is a much easier, faster way to get through the noise, get their attention, and set up an interview. With text messaging it's easier than ever to send a quick follow-up thank-you message and ask for the next step. Here's what you do:

1. During your conversation, when you make the vague agreement to meet sometime in the future, casually ask for your prospect's phone number and say, "Sounds good. I'll text you my contact information so we can get together." (It is highly unlikely they'll protest if your conversation has been positive.)

2. As soon as you walk away from the conversation, send a social media connection request (*if appropriate*). This continues the process of building familiarity and, if your prospect accepts, opens up another communication channel.

3. Within 24 hours, send a text message thanking them for the conversation and request a meeting. Personalize it with information you gleaned during your conversation.

4. If you don't get a response, try sending your text again a day later. In some cases, they won't recognize your phone number and will ignore your initial attempt. They may also be busy and don't get to it.

5. If your second attempt fails, shift to the phone and e-mail to make contact. It serves no purpose to create potential ill will by continuing to text.

Use Text to Nurture Prospects

Text messaging can play an integral role in nurturing prospects with whom you have a relationship but are not in the WEO or ready to make a commitment. A quick, value-added text message is an easy way to keep top of mind without seeming too intrusive.

For example, Petty Officer Second Class Burdett systematically leverages four prospecting channels—phone, e-mail, social, and text. He calls once a quarter to find out how his prospects are doing. He supplements those calls with monthly e-mails, direct messages, and text messages with links to articles and news about the Navy or sports or other things his prospects are interested in. He also follows his prospects on social media and, when appropriate, likes and shares their posts.

Burdett's text message strategy works brilliantly. He reserves his best value-added information for text messages. Because he is familiar with his prospects' interests and motivations, he often texts links to relevant articles, memes, and videos that he knows will grab their attention and interest. This often creates a short back-and-forth dialogue on an area of interest, which, in turn, maintains a connection with his best prospects.

Burdett's strategy keeps his prospects engaged and nurtures the relationship. His text messages are appreciated and nonintrusive because they are valuable and personalized. Because of this, Burdett is always top of mind when his prospects are considering education and career paths.

Use Text to Create Opportunities for Engagement

Text messages are also well received when they make your prospect feel important. Short text messages sent to congratulate them on a milestone, an achievement, a sports team win, an individual accomplishment, an award or recognition, or something they posted on social media will get their attention.

Engagement text messages usually get a positive response as long as they are sincere, personalized, and free of direct solicitations for anything. The goal is simple: Give your prospect a reason to engage you in a conversation. You increase this possibility by making them feel important.

Seven Rules for Structuring Effective Text Prospecting Messages

For your text message to be effective, you need to engage your prospect and get them to take action in the blink of an eye. Packing your message into a small space requires you to be thoughtful, creative, and focused. It's difficult to make an impact in 200 characters or less. There are seven rules for effective text messages:

1. **Identify yourself.** Never take for granted that your prospect has your information saved on their phone. As a best practice, include your name, rank, and branch at the top of the message. Example: [FROM—Jeb Blount—Fanatical Military Recruiting]

2. **Message matters.** What you say and how you say it carries impact. Be very careful that your tone is not misinterpreted in a negative way. Use complete sentences to avoid sounding abrupt, harsh, sarcastic, or flippant. Keep it professional at all times.

3. **Be direct—be brief.** Say exactly what you mean in clear, precise, well-written sentences using good grammar and spelling. Remember that this is a professional message and you are an NCO in the United States Military. Keep the text to one to four short sentences and less than 200 characters when possible. Avoid rambling, run-on sentences. Avoid using emoticons (some are inappropriate), and most important, you must be professional.

4. **Avoid abbreviations.** Avoid using abbreviations on text messages to prospects. Abbreviations like LOL, OMG, WTF, and others don't come off as professional. Likewise, you should avoid acronyms and slang. Yes, I know that the folks you are texting use a lot of abbreviation. Yes, I know that you do the same with your friends and family. But this is not appropriate for professional text messages, and you don't know who you might offend with a wrong abbreviation or who else (parents) may be reading your message.

5. **Use transparent links.** People are extremely suspicious of shortened hyperlinks. When you send URLs to prospects that link to articles or other resources, send the entire URL so they know where they are clicking.

6. **Before clicking "send"—pause and read it again.** Make this your rule when it comes to text messages (and, frankly, all written communications).

7. **Know your numbers.** Finally, as with all prospecting channels, know your numbers. Track the number of texts you send each day, the response rates, the conversions into interviews and, ultimately, enlistments.

Do not text while driving—put the smartphone down!

24

E-Mail and Direct Messaging

Your e-mail inbox is a bit like a Las Vegas roulette machine. You know, you just check it and check it, and every once in a while there's some juicy little tidbit of reward, like the three quarters that pop down on a one-armed bandit. And that keeps you coming back for more.

—Douglas Rushkoff, writer

E-mail and social media direct messaging are powerful parts of a balanced prospecting approach. Most of your prospects will have an e-mail account and almost all of them will have a social media in-box that allows you to send a direct message.

Facebook Messenger, Instagram, Twitter, LinkedIn, WhatsApp, and Snapchat are often used as proxies, supplements, or complete replacements for traditional e-mail. The benefit of the social media channel and direct messaging (DM) apps is that you may send mail to prospects even if you don't know their e-mail address (though in most cases you need to be connected with them first).

The downside of direct messages and e-mail, in all forms, is that if you irritate your prospect by sending them spam-laden crap, they'll block you, spam you, or unfriend you in a heartbeat. E-mail done wrong wastes your time, makes you look unprofessional, and exasperates prospects.

When leveraged intelligently, though, e-mail and direct messages engage and open conversations with prospects. E-mail done right is a powerful prospecting methodology that will reward you with a consistent stream of qualified prospects.

In this chapter you'll learn a simple four-step framework that will instantly make your prospecting e-mails and DMs on social media more impactful and improve conversion.

The Four Cardinal Rules of E-Mail and Direct Message Prospecting

Message matters. Effective e-mail and direct message prospecting requires thoughtfulness and effort and begins with four cardinal rules (see Figure 24.1).

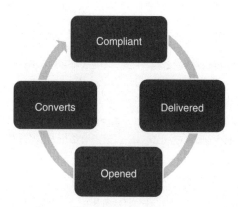

Figure 24.1   Four Cardinal Rules of E-Mail and Direct Message Prospecting

Rule #1: *Your E-Mail Must Get Delivered*

If your message doesn't get delivered you have no chance for conversion and you've wasted your time. Most individuals today have filters set up that either block or move "spam" e-mails to a junk folder. They may also block you from DMing them on social media.

There is no perfect science that lets you stay completely clear of spam filters. The good news is that your government e-mail address is likely to be whitelisted by most e-mail service providers, so e-mail you send will get through.

You can do additional things to increase the probability that your e-mail gets delivered. This is not a comprehensive list—rather, it's a list of the most obvious and important tactics.

- **Don't send bulk e-mail.** Prospecting e-mail is one to one. It is one e-mail from your address sent to one individual, one e-mail at a time. This alone should help you clear 90 percent of spam hurdles. Sending bulk e-mail (the same message to multiple people) from your personal e-mail address is the easiest and fastest way to get blacklisted, get blocked, and look like a total imbecile. The same goes for creating groups on Messenger and blasting those groups.
- **Avoid attaching images**. Because hackers and spammers embed malware in images, many e-mail programs mark e-mails with images as spam or block images until permission is given to download. Your best bet on prospecting e-mails is to avoid sending images. This is not the case, however, with social in-boxes.
- **Avoid hyperlinks.** The primary tool of hackers is the hyperlink. You click on it, and the hacker inserts malware on your computer and steals your information. Because of this, people are super suspicious of hyperlinks embedded in e-mails and DMs. Your best bet is to avoid hyperlinks altogether in prospecting e-mails because they also trigger spam filters. If you do include a link:
  - Avoid embedding the URL in text.
  - Include the entire URL for complete transparency.

- Avoid shortened URLs that obscure the website address.
- Limit the total number of URLs to one—including any links in your e-mail signature.

■ **Avoid attachments.** Hackers have become adept at using attachments to infect computers with malware, hack websites, and infiltrate networks. Because of this danger, spam filters may block your e-mail if it contains attachments. Your best bet is to avoid sending attachments in prospecting e-mails.

■ **Skip spammy words and phrases.** What you say and how you say it can trigger spam filters. For example, using ALL CAPS in a subject line, adding exclamation points, or using words like *free* or *cash* can light up spam filters like a Christmas tree. Be careful and thoughtful about the symbols and words you use and how you phrase those words—especially in your e-mail subject line. The best thing to do is step into the spammer's shoes—look at the annoying spam you get and then do the opposite.

■ **Don't send too many e-mails or DMs to the same person.** This may seem counterintuitive, but with e-mail and direct messages, too much persistence can hurt you. If you become annoying, the recipient of your e-mail can mark it as spam or block you altogether.

■ **Scrub bounces.** Many e-mail filters will block you if you send multiple e-mails to an e-mail address that doesn't exist. When you get a bounce, view it as an opportunity to gather better information. Update the contact in your Recruiting Information Support System and remove the e-mail address so you won't mistakenly send to that address again. Then get to work by phone or in person to get an accurate e-mail address.

Rule #2: Your E-Mail Must Get Opened

Here's a fact of life: People get a lot of e-mail, and there is simply no way they can possibly get to it all. Your prospects cope with being overwhelmed by an in-box that is set to "infinite refill" the same way you do: *scan and triage*. They, like you, must make split-second decisions to open, delete, or save for later. To get opened, your prospecting e-mail or direct message must stand out from all of the noise and be compelling enough to entice a click.

- **Familiarity gets your e-mail opened.** One way to stand out is familiarity. Imagine that you are scanning your in-box. An e-mail or DM from a person you recognize catches your eye. What is the your most probable next action?

  The law of familiarity is always in play with e-mail and direct message prospecting. The more familiar your prospect is with you, the more likely they are to open your e-mail. This is why leveraging the phone and both face-to-face and social channels before sending an e-mail or DM can increase the chances of getting your message opened.

  The layering of channels to build familiarity is powerful. For example, after meeting your prospect at an event, you might send a text, leave a voice mail, "like" something your prospect posts on Facebook, and follow that up with a DM and/or e-mail. This increases familiarity and the probability that your prospect will respond.

  Layering prospecting channels should be focused, targeted, intentional, and strategic. You need to plan your touches across the various prospecting channels to improve opening rates for your e-mail and direct messages without becoming annoying.
- **Your subject line must scream "open me!"** Depending on the level of familiarity your prospect has with you, the subject line can be the most important key to getting your e-mail opened. Sadly, though, most prospecting e-mail subject lines neither stand out nor are compelling. Most, in fact, scream "delete me!"

These are the three most common subject line mistakes:

1. **They're too long.** Data from many sources prove that shorter subject lines outperform longer subject lines by wide margins. Frankly, it's intuitive. A long subject line requires your prospect's brain to work harder. In the context of split-second decisions about the value of an e-mail, that extra effort gets you deleted.

Most of the e-mail messages you send your prospects will be opened on a mobile device. If you consider your own behavior on your mobile phone, you are quicker to delete a message there. Put more than 50 characters in your subject line, and the open rate goes down exponentially.

Solution: Keep e-mail prospecting subject lines super short—three to six words or 40 to 50 characters including spaces. Remember—less is more.

2. **They include questions.** E-mail prospecting subject lines in the form of questions are delete bait. Virtually every major study conducted on the efficacy of different types of e-mail subject lines has concluded that subject lines in the form of a question quickly doom your e-mail to the delete-button death-roll. Though there may be a time and place for using a question in your e-mail subject line, in most cases you should step away from the question mark.

Solution: Use action words and directive statements instead of questions. List-based subject lines that include a testimonial like "Three Reasons Why a Military Career Will Make You Stronger" are especially powerful, as are referral subject lines like "Jeb Blount Said We Should Talk" and statement-based subject lines like "Adventure Awaits You."

3. **They're impersonal or boring.** Generic, impersonal subject lines—usually ones that are about you and your branch—are boring. When you are attempting to engage prospects—especially overstimulated teenagers—a failure to grab their attention will send you straight to the trash.

Think about it. Every recruiter in the military, colleges, and the private sector is trying to connect with the highest-value prospects in your market. These top prospects are inundated with requests for interviews and meetings. You will never break through this noise and get their attention with boring, cheesy, or impersonal subject lines. Instead of standing out, you'll just be another person junking up your prospect's in-box and wasting their time.

Solution: Connect your subject line to an issue your prospect is facing—especially if it is emotional or stressful—or compliment them on a recent accomplishment or something that you know makes them feel proud. For example, the easiest, fastest way to get me to open your e-mail is a subject line that reads: "Loved Your Book!" You can also use relevant humor or tongue-in-cheek phrases to catch your prospect's attention when appropriate.

We are all self-centered and almost always focused on our own problems, issues, accomplishments, and ego. The fact is, 95 percent of the time we are thinking about ourselves, and the 5 percent of time that we are not thinking about ourselves, something—maybe a mouthy recruiter—has gotten in the way of us thinking about ourselves.

So play the odds, and make your subject line about your prospect. It's really easy to do if you take a little extra time to research the recipient of your prospecting e-mail.

The brutal reality, though, is there is no secret formula for creating the perfect e-mail subject line every time. What works with one group of prospects may not work with another. This is why experimentation and testing are the real secrets to success with subject lines.

Testing helps you zero in on which subject lines get the most opens. With this data in hand, you'll often find patterns that lead to subject lines that work phenomenally well with certain prospect groups.

Yet most recruiters don't test. Instead, they create subject lines on the fly and then send their e-mails into a black hole, hoping that they'll get a response. It's an incredibly frustrating way to prospect because it's like throwing darts at a target while blindfolded and hoping you hit a bull's-eye, without any feedback to let you know if your aim is true.

With this information, you'll be able to narrow down and home in on the words and phrases that get the best response, and your e-mails will stand out and get opened.

Rule #3: Your E-Mail Must Convert

Unless you are sending pure spam—generic e-mail and DM templates that are copied and pasted, then sent randomly to a large swath of prospects regardless of relevance and with no research—developing and crafting effective messaging requires a significant investment in time.

To engage highest-qualified prospects, you will need to personalize each e-mail message. Thought and effort will be required to craft a relevant e-mail that connects with the most desirable prospects and moves them to take action.

This doesn't mean that every e-mail you send must be built from scratch. Certainly, within specific targeted demographics there will be enough common ground and patterns that you'll be able to develop templates that can be easily customized. These customizable templates allow you to deliver more prospecting e-mail and DM touches in a shorter period of time.

Even with a customizable template, though, to be effective, you must do research so the message looks and feels unique to the recipient. It will fall on deaf ears if the recipient doesn't feel that it was crafted specifically for them.

This costly investment of your precious and limited time is why it is imperative that your prospecting e-mails and DMs convert. In other words, generating a response that leads to your desired outcome:

- An interview
- Connecting with you on social media
- Qualifying information
- Accepting an invite to meet you at an event
- Viewing a video or clicking on a link
- A recruiting conversation

If your message doesn't compel the recipient to take action, your time and effort were wasted. This is why investing the time to get your message right is critical.

Rule #4: Your E-Mail Must Be Compliant

There are rules and laws governing e-mail communication. Ensure that you know and comply with regulations.

Effective Prospecting E-Mail and Direct Messages Begins with a Plan

A plan helps you define who will be getting your e-mail, the method or technique you will use to get their attention, the message you will craft to connect with them and compel them to take action, and finally, the action you want the recipient to take. With e-mail and DM prospecting, this is your AMMO (see Figure 24.2):

You don't have to look far to see that planning is rare when it comes to prospecting messages. The vast majority of prospecting e-mail and DMs are awful.

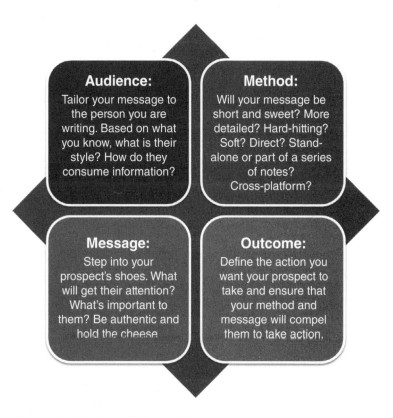

Audience:
Tailor your message to the person you are writing. Based on what you know, what is their style? How do they consume information?

Method:
Will your message be short and sweet? More detailed? Hard-hitting? Soft? Direct? Stand-alone or part of a series of notes? Cross-platform?

Message:
Step into your prospect's shoes. What will get their attention? What's important to them? Be authentic and hold the cheese.

Outcome:
Define the action you want your prospect to take and ensure that your method and message will compel them to take action.

Figure 24.2   E-mail AMMO

Because I am a business owner and decision maker, I get blasted by prospecting e-mails and direct messages from every direction—on my work e-mail, LinkedIn, Twitter, and Facebook. I receive dozens each week that are laughable and embarrassments to the people who sent them.

I'm baffled at how often people who took the time to send a message to me did no research. Bad e-mail and DM messages destroy your personal brand equity, credibility, and image. The worst messages are:

- Long, important-sounding pitches using incomprehensible jargon—a lot of words with no meaning
- Feature dumps
- Cheerleaders who write over and over about how great they are
- The ones that get my name wrong—seriously, it is Jeb: three letters
- The long ones that cause eyes to glaze over. WTF, we live in the age of Twitter, text messaging, infographics, OMGs, and LOLs. Prospects have the attention span of mosquitos.

I delete 99.9 percent of them.

Every once in a while, though, I'll get a brilliant e-mail or DM that makes me stop in my tracks. This golden message connects with me, makes sense, is relevant, and compels me to respond. The sender took time to research and plan.

In our competitive marketplace, where talented people are in demand and have many options, in order to get their attention, message matters.

Consider your *audience*. Prospects are people—not robots—so your message should be authentic and personal. It should connect emotionally. You need to ensure that the tone, structure, and formality of your message is a match for the person you are writing. The emotional connection is vital because your e-mail or DM will be effective only if it causes your prospect to take an intended action.

Determine your *method.* Will you leverage a single, standalone e-mail or DM or a multi-message campaign? The method you choose should be driven by your intended audience and defined outcome:

- Standalone?
- Part of a campaign?
- Nurturing or action oriented?
- Cross-platform?

This is where planning and strategy are crucial—especially with Alpha prospects. You want to avoid being random with your most important opportunities.

Tailor the *message* **to your audience.** The message you craft must be strong enough to compel your prospect to take action. Your prospect wants to know that you get them and their problems, so your message must be relevant to their situation. The most effective way to tailor your message to the person you are writing is to step into their shoes:

- What will get their attention?
- Short and sweet?
- More detailed?
- Hard-hitting?
- Soft?
- Direct?
- What's important to them?
- What will cause them to give you what you are asking for?

The key here is taking time to do basic research to get to know your prospect and using that information as the foundation on which you construct your message.

Define your desired *outcome.* If you don't know what you want, you won't get what you want. If you fail to clearly define what you are asking your prospect to do or provide, they will be confused.

The Four-Step E-mail Prospecting Framework

The AMMO framework assists you in planning and developing your strategy. Once you have your plan in place, you'll use the *Four-Step E-mail Prospecting Framework* to craft your e-mail (see Figure 24.3):

1. **Hook:** Get their attention with a compelling subject line and opening sentence/statement.
2. **Relate:** Demonstrate that you get them and their problem. Show empathy and authenticity.
3. **Bridge:** Connect the dots between their problem and how you can help them. Explain the WIIFM.
4. **Ask:** Be clear and straightforward about the action you want them to take, and make it easy for them to do so.

Here is an example of a message to a prior service prospect that leverages the four-step framework:

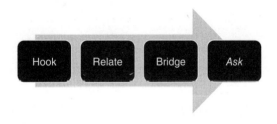

Figure 24.3 Four Step E-mail Prospecting Framework

Subject: This is why you miss wearing the uniform

Dave,

It's 1400 hours and you're patrolling in 120-degree weather with 60 pounds of gear on your shoulders. Life sucks! Or does it?

For many of us that have moved on, these are our best stories. Most start with, "No shit, so there I was. . ." There is nothing like the camaraderie that you get being next to your friends embracing the suck.

The civilian world can be stressful, lonely, and not all that it's cracked up to be. I help veterans like you get back to a way of life that gives you a sense of pride and connection every time you put on the uniform. Whether it's full or part-time, you can get back to playing with guns and blowing stuff up (who doesn't like that?).

While I don't know if the Army is still a good fit for you, why don't we get together, so I can learn more about you and what you miss the most? From there, we can decide if it makes sense to keep talking. I'm going to be in your neck of the woods on Wednesday. Why don't we meet for lunch?

SSG Early, United States Army

Hook

You have about three seconds to grab your prospect's attention and hook them. In that three seconds, your subject line must compel them to open the e-mail, and the first sentence (especially with direct messages on social where there is no subject line) must entice them to keep reading.

Prospects choose to read your e-mail and DMs for their reasons, not yours. Therefore, the best way to hook them is to make your subject line relevant and the opening sentence about them. You must step into their shoes and focus on their unique situation and interests. Let's take a look at our model e-mail:

> **Subject: *This is why you miss wearing the uniform***
>
> **First Sentence:** It's 1400 hours and you're patrolling in 120-degree weather with 60 pounds of gear on your shoulders. Life sucks! Or does it?

We are writing to a *prior service prospect*. Both the subject line and the first sentence are emotional. We are connecting with why Dave feels like he's missing something in his life since leaving the Army.

Relate

Effective messages connect with prospects on an emotional level. The reason is simple: People make decisions based on emotion. The easiest way to connect with your prospect emotionally is to demonstrate that you get them and their problems. You connect when you demonstrate that you can relate to their struggles and issues.

Our second paragraph steps into Dave's shoes and lets him know that we get him. The message is authentic and genuine.

> For many of us that have moved on, these are our best stories. Most start with, "No shit, so there I was. . ." There is nothing like the camaraderie that you get being next to your friends embracing the suck.

Bridge

Since prospects do things for their reasons, not yours, you must answer their most pressing question: "If I give you what you want— my time—*what's in it for me?*" If you are unable to answer WIIFM with value that exceeds the cost of your prospect giving up their time, your message will not convert.

This is where your research pays off. When you know a specific issue that your prospect is facing, you should bridge directly to that issue and how you might be able to solve it. When you are unsure of a specific issue, bridge to issues that are common to your prospect's situation.

> The civilian world can be stressful, lonely, and not all that it's cracked up to be. I help veterans like you get back to a way of life that gives you a sense of pride and connection every time you put on the uniform. Whether it's full or part-time, you can get back to playing with guns and blowing stuff up (who doesn't like that?).

We've tied our subject line, opening sentence, and relate statement together with a bridge that connects the dots between Dave's (potential) disenchantment with the civilian world and solutions that reduce stress. We've answered Dave's WIIFM question.

Most importantly, we are speaking Dave's language—pride, connection, camaraderie, certainty, fulfillment, and fun. By speaking Dave's language, we continue to relate and demonstrate that we get him and his problems.

Ask

To get what you want, you ask for what you want—assumptively, assertively, and confidently.

> While I don't know if the Army is still a good fit for you,
> why don't we get together, so I can learn more about you
> and what you miss the most? From there, we can decide if it
> makes sense to keep talking. I'm going to be in your neck of
> the woods on Wednesday. Why don't we meet for lunch?

Notice how we leverage a subtle takeaway—"While I don't know if the Army is still a good fit for you . . ." This non-complementary behavior disrupts expectations. Telling Dave up front that this might not be a good fit is exactly the opposite of what he would expect of a recruiter. Unlike pitching that pushes prospects away, disrupting expectations (pattern painting) pulls prospects toward you.

Then we send a subtle but powerful message. We tell him that we want to *learn* more about *him* and *listen* to *his* story. This pulls Dave in deeper because everyone wants to be heard. We love to tell our story to people who are willing to listen.

Finally, we remove the stress and pressure. If it doesn't make sense, "I'm not going to push things." It's just a short conversation to see if we should keep talking.

Then we assumptively ("How about") ask for a meeting and offer a day and time, which takes the burden off Dave to make that decision.

Here are a couple of additional examples:

> ### Subject: High school is over but it feels like something is missing
>
> Alicia,
>   You've been out of high school for a few months now working hard to make your own way in the world. But it's tough out there with low-paying jobs, college debt, and the high cost of everything. It feels like something is missing.

This is why so many talented people like you are taking a second look at career opportunities in the military. We offer exceptional pay and benefits, including housing, meals, medical, and education.

A military career is a fast track to financial peace of mind, travel and adventure, the pride that comes with serving your country, and friendships that will last a lifetime. But we are an exclusive club. Not everyone qualifies.

Why don't we schedule a short call to help me learn more about you and your goals? From there, we can decide together if it makes sense to keep talking. How about Tuesday at 10:00 a.m.?

PO2 Early, United States Navy

Subject: The biggest threat to your future is college loan debt

Jeremy,

With graduation coming up soon, you've got big choices to make. I can't even imagine what it must be like standing in your shoes.

CNN recently reported that the average college graduate leaves school with more than $30,000 in loan debt. Yet many college graduates are struggling to find high-paying jobs. Nobody wants to spend four years in college only to end up saddled with student debt and few job opportunities.

The good news is skilled trades are on the rise, and employers cannot find enough trained employees to fill the positions. Salary.com reports that the average aircraft mechanic makes $83,523 in the United States and Glassdoor reports that the average entry-level cybersecurity analyst makes approximately $94,490.

I help talented people like you get paid while training. You'll gain valuable experience in high-paying trades like these, and that makes you extremely marketable.

Although I'm not sure if you even qualify for the op-portunities offered by the military, I thought the best place to begin is a short call to help me learn more about you and your interests. From there, if it makes sense, we can set up a time to have a deeper conversation. How about Wednesday at 5:30 p.m.?

MSgt Early, United States Air Force

Practice, Practice, Practice

Writing effective e-mail and DM prospecting messages is not easy. The most difficult step is training yourself to step into your pros-pect's shoes, relate to their situation, and learn to speak their lan-guage. Stop focusing on what you want and what you have to offer, and instead develop the habit of researching prospects and focusing on issues they are facing.

You will struggle at first. Everybody does. The key is practicing until effective, authentic e-mail messages roll off your fingertips. The more you practice, the faster and more proficient you will become at writing prospecting messages that convert.

Pause Before You Press "Send"

I am the typo king. I'm quite sure you may have found a few of my mistakes while reading this book. So I end this chapter with humble advice from a man who has made the terrible mistake of not pausing before pushing "send" and launching a typo-, misspelling-, and grammatical-error-laden message to a prospect. It is a lesson you want to avoid learning the hard way.

Proof your prospecting e-mail before you send it. Run it through spell and grammar check on your computer. Read it once. Read it twice. Print the really important e-mails and proof the hard copy. Step away from it for 10 minutes and read it again (you'll be amazed at what you catch using this process).

Your e-mail is a reflection of you, your professionalism, and your personal brand. Pause before you push "send" to ensure that the impression you make is a positive one.

25 | Social Recruiting

Social media is an amazing tool, but it's really the face-to-face interaction that makes a long-term impact.

—Felicia Day, actress

The influence of social media on recruiting is inescapable. Millions of people are linked together on social media sites—constantly checking and updating their status. As a recruiting tool, social media has moved from cutting edge to ubiquitous and inextricably woven into the fabric of military recruiting.

The social channel is a key component of a balanced prospecting methodology. There has never been a time in history when so much information about so many prospects was so easy to access.

Not just contact information, but context. Through the window of social media, you can:

- Gain glimpses into your prospect's behavior, motivations, desires, preferences, and triggers that drive career decisions and preferences.
- Easily uncover interests that lead to more impactful and robust face-to-face conversations.
- Build familiarity through low-impact, nonintrusive techniques that you may communicate seamlessly via the social in-box.

Social Recruiting Is Not a Panacea

Along with the increased awareness of the power of the social channel, there is a disturbing trend of recruiters using social media as a substitute and excuse for avoiding telephone and face-to-face prospecting. It's easier to hide out on Facebook or Instagram all day than to interrupt strangers and engage in human-to-human conversations.

Social media is an important piece of the prospecting puzzle, but it is not a panacea. Contact and conversion rates from phone, face-to-face, and text message prospecting dwarf conversion rates on social media.

The social channel enhances, elevates, and sometimes accelerates your prospecting efforts. It certainly moves you into your prospect's familiarity bubble. But it is not a replacement for focused and deliberate outbound prospecting efforts.

The Social Recruiting Challenge

From time to time, though, a recruiter will challenge me on this premise. It happens in most FMR training classes. As we start talking about the power, efficiency, and effectiveness of telephone prospecting, I'll notice a recruiter who sinks lower and lower in his seat and avoids eye contact.

I call them out: "Sargent Echols, it looks to me like you aren't buying this?" The response is always the same.

"I know you say the phone works, and maybe it does for other people, but I get far better results on social media (Facebook, Snapchat, Instagram, Twitter). Besides, no one answers the phone anymore."

He'll usually go on with a long-winded justification for why spending all day online is far more effective that talking to actual prospects. Sometimes he'll throw out the words "old school" just for good measure.

I never fail to notice the incredulous looks on the faces of his leaders who are sitting behind him. They know the truth, and so do I. This recruiter rarely, if ever, makes mission.

If you think social media is magic fairy dust that will allow you to avoid the hard work of prospecting, you are in for a rude awakening.

Social recruiting will not solve your pipeline woes and provide an endless stream of qualified prospects with little effort. It takes far more than a Facebook connection and hope to move today's talented young Americans to take action.

Social Recruiting Is About Nuance

Let's get this straight from the get-go. People don't want to be pitched or "sold" on social media. They prefer to connect, interact, and learn. For this reason, the social channel is better suited to building familiarity, nurturing a lead, research, nuanced inbound prospecting, and trigger-event awareness.

This is why effective social recruiting is a long, hard slog. It takes daily, ongoing, consistent effort. It requires you to think, manage your message, and be present. If you are truly activating social media as a part of your balanced prospecting arsenal, you know that the commitment to consistency can be exhausting.

With the exception of the social in-box, which can be a supplement and alternative to the traditional e-mail in-box, social recruiting is about nuance, tact, and patience.

Social recruiting is a collective term that encompasses a variety of activities—all designed to enrich the recruiting process and fill the pipe with more qualified and motivated prospects. These activities include:

- Social research
- Social networking
- Social inbound marketing
- Social prospecting
- Social trigger-event monitoring

It's critical that you integrate social media in your balanced prospecting arsenal and work to become a master at leveraging the social channel.

Choosing the Right Social Channels

Because the social media landscape is changing and continues to change so rapidly, I am going to avoid diving into the specific features/tactics of the major social media sites and tools. Frankly, because the social media sites are so feature rich, it would require several more books to give you everything you'd ever need to know, and by the time those books were published, they'd all be out of date.

The social media landscape is complex. The task of mastering and getting engaged on social media is daunting and frankly overwhelming—so much so that most organizations have an entire team of people assigned to manage their social media presence. That's how much effort it takes.

As an individual recruiter, there's no way you can maintain a consistent cadence on every social channel and still have time to manage the recruiting process. Should you try to keep up a presence on all of these channels, you'll find that it is exhausting.

What's more, the fickle nature of teenagers means that social media channels are in and out of favor like the wind. It's a moving target.

I've found that I can effectively manage three channels at a time, and I'm much better when I'm only working two. Beyond that it gets tedious, and my efforts are diluted. Take a step back and answer these two questions:

1. On which social channels are my prospects engaged?
2. On which social channels do I feel most comfortable?

The ROI on your social recruiting efforts will increase significantly if you are playing in the same sandbox as your prospects (students, grads, and prior service).

It's also important to engage in channels you're comfortable with and enjoy. For example, I spend a lot of time on Twitter because I love it. My audience spans almost all of the major channels, but Twitter is by far my favorite, and it shows in my follower base (follow me @salesgravy).

Five Objectives of Social Recruiting

Do you hear that giant sucking sound? That is social media stealing Golden Hour time from recruiters across all branches of the military. Hours upon hours of prime recruiting time wasted with heads stuck in laptops, tablets, and smartphones—"social recruiting."

The social channel is mesmerizing and addictive. It is designed to be that way, to hook you so you keep coming back for more. That's why those likes, shares, hearts, notices, and little numbers on the social apps on your phone exist. They trigger your curiosity, need for significance, and competitiveness.

Social media is a big money-making machine that devours your data, time, and attention, and sells it to advertisers. To do that, it needs you to be hooked. When you spend your entire day on social media, don't think for a minute that it is any different from parking yourself in front of a TV screen.

Of course, the difference between television and the social channel is that you can actually accomplish something on social media when you gain the discipline to focus your time on creating specific outcomes that help you identify prospects and move them into the recruiting pipeline and applicant funnel.

You must learn to use social media the right way, so it is a good use of time. *Efficient* and *effective* is the name of the game. Your time investment in the social channel must be focused on increasing the size and viability of your recruiting pipeline and moving applicants into the funnel. Otherwise you're just wasting time. Table 25.1 shows Social Recruiting Objectives and the Five Cs of Social Recruiting

Table 25.1   The Five Objectives of Social Recruiting and The Five Cs of Social Recruiting

Five Objectives of Social Recruiting (Outcomes)	The Five Cs of the Social Recruiting Process (Effective)
Personal Branding	Connecting
Marketing, Education, and Insights	Content Creation
WEO Awareness	Content Curation
Research and Information Gathering	Conversion
Outbound Prospecting via Direct Engagement	Consistency

Personal Branding

Here are two questions you must constantly be asking yourself as you engage in social recruiting:

1. Does my presence online support my efforts to build my reputation as a military recruiter of integrity who can be trusted?
2. Does my presence online help people become familiar with my name, personal brand, and my branch of the United States Armed Forces in a positive way?

If the answer to either of these questions is "no" or "I'm not sure," it's time to make an adjustment in your strategy. The primary objective of social recruiting is building familiarity and trust. You want to be seen, heard, and perceived as a credible resource for potential applicants.

At a basic level, prospects will look you up online to get the gist of who you are and what you are all about before meeting with you. What they find will cause them to make instant judgments about you. Those judgments will impact your ability to influence and persuade them to engage. Your professional presence online should position you as the one person who is most capable of helping prospects gain valuable insight into a career in the military.

Like most people, you make quick judgments or build quick impressions about others when you are introduced for the first time. That is just how we operate as human beings. With so much incoming data attacking our nervous system, our brains have evolved to quickly grab available information about others (how they look, talk, act) and compile that information into a snapshot of that person. Those first impressions—regardless of how valid they are—influence our feelings toward the other person.

True, in the physical world you sometimes get a second chance to make a good first impression. In the virtual world, however, you have zero chance of changing first impressions that are made about you online. When prospects view the "online you" and don't like what they see, they just move on.

The most common mistakes recruiters make that damage their personal brand online are:

- Poorly written profiles
- Incomplete and outdated profiles
- Unprofessional photo or no photo
- Opinionated political or religious postings and discussions
- TMI—too much information about personal issues

Your social media profiles are a direct reflection of your personal brand. These profiles are the tip of the social recruiting spear. Until your prospect (and their parents) meet you, who you are online is who you are. This is why it is critical that you invest time in developing and perfecting your social profiles.

Today, not tomorrow, take action to ensure that your online image casts you in the best light. Here are some of the basics:

- **Headshot**—According to PhotoFeeler.com, a website that helps people choose the right photo for online profiles, "Profile photos are so essential to modern communication that a good one's become a basic necessity. And that couldn't be truer than for those of us whose professional lives are tied to social media profiles."

  Ensure that you have a professional headshot, *in uniform*, on all your social profiles. Professional means you leave your cat, dog, kids, vacation, college buddies, cool sunglasses, and bottle of beer out of the picture. Make sure the picture is taken in good light at a flattering angle and has a neutral background. Lose the cheesy poses—like with your arms crossed, hand on your chin, or cocking your eyeglasses. You don't want to come off looking like a schmuck.

  Instead, smile and put a pleasant look on your face. In a study[1] based on over 60,000 ratings, Photo Feeler found that a genuine smile has a significant impact on other people's perceptions of your competence, likability, and influence based on your profile picture.

A best practice that I highly recommend is posting the same headshot on all of your social media profiles. Your image is like your logo. You want it to stick.

- **Cover image**—Inbound marketing juggernaut HubSpot.com advises that "having a social media profile without a cover photo is like having a brick-and-mortar business without a store sign."

  Most social media sites allow you to upload a cover image (sometimes called a hero image) to your profile. This is, most often, a background placed on the header. It is a free way to let an image tell your story.

  Make sure you have a professional cover image on all of your social profiles. The image dimensions and specs for each social network are different and change often. You'll find dozens of resources online that provide detailed information on cover images. You don't need to be a graphic artist to craft a good cover image. I recommend using Canva.com—a free graphics website that makes it easy to build your social profile cover.

- **Summary/bio/about you**—Personal branding expert William Arruda says that "an effective [social media] summary makes people want to know more about you and ultimately connect with you one-on-one." This is also true of the "about you" and bio sections on each of your social media profiles. You can go long form on Facebook, LinkedIn, and YouTube and get creative with short and sweet descriptions on Twitter, Instagram, and Snapchat.

  Writing a perfect summary that connects with prospects, parents, educators, administrators, and community partners requires thoughtfulness. It's your story. It should be well written, truthful, and compelling enough that after reading it people want to engage with you and meet you.

  Write in the first person and make it conversational. Your bio should explain who you are, what you are all about (values), your accomplishments, career milestones, and why you love being a part of the military.

- **Contact information**—You are in recruiting. Your job is to engage qualified prospects and move them into the recruiting funnel. The very best thing that can happen is a prospect who calls and interrupts *you*. If you make it hard for them, they won't. If you don't provide contact information, they can't.

  So make it easy. Put your contact information, including recruiting phone and e-mail, on your social media profiles as appropriate *and in compliance with regulations.*

- **Media and links**—Ensure that you are cross-linking each social media profile page to your other profile pages and branch websites. Regularly post rich media, including photos, links to relevant articles, podcasts, and videos. Take the time to add information that will be interesting to your prospects, educate them, and give them a reason to connect with you.

- **Custom URLs**—Most social media sites will allow you to create a custom URL for your page. A custom URL makes it easier for people to find you and to share your profile.

- **Update your profiles regularly**—Make a commitment to manage your online presence by reviewing, updating, and continuously improving all of your online profiles at least once a quarter. Things change. Make sure your profiles are changing with you and that they stay fresh. As you review your online profiles, answer this question: Based purely on the information on your social profile, would *you* enlist with you?

Building Familiarity

The social channel is the most efficient and effective way to build familiarity. To build familiarity, you must be present and consistently engaging with prospects online. The more prospects see you, the more they like you and become comfortable with you.

Engaging means liking, sharing, and *appropriately* commenting on your prospect's posts as well as content they are commenting on and sharing. You also need to post content that is of interest to them and congratulate them on achievements.

Be aware that you are always onstage. Everything, from your profile picture to the things you post, like, share, and comment on, are being watched by prospects and their circle of influence, so it's critical that you manage your message.

We live in a hypersensitive world. People are easily offended by the smallest things. The wrong words, wrong like, or wrong comment can damage your reputation and personal brand; in extreme cases they can go viral and derail your career.

Familiarity is a two-edged sword. When impressions of you are positive, familiarity can cut through friction and help you initiate recruiting conversations with prospects. But when prospects have a negative impression of you, they will erect walls to keep you out.

This is simple. Think before you post. If you think what you are posting could be controversial in any way, shape, or form, sit on it for 24 hours before pushing the post button.

Marketing Through Insight and Education

The very best outcome of the investment you make in social media is to entice prospects to contact you. An inbound lead is much easier to qualify and convert into an interview than an outbound prospecting call. Inbound prospects are also excellent resources for referrals.

Familiarity plays a key but passive role in inbound prospecting. When you are well known to prospects, they will often contact you when trigger events cause them to begin thinking about career choices.

Sharing and publishing relevant content that is intriguing to prospects and helps them solve problems, answering questions in groups, and posting thoughtful comments can also open the door to prospects contacting you for more information or to ask you questions—especially when these posts demonstrate empathy and position you as a trustworthy resource.

It's also a good idea to consistently post content on careers in the military, military success stories, links to information about military career choices, general updates on community and school events, and other content that pulls people in and positions you as an expert.

WEO Awareness

Windows of Enlistment Opportunity (WEO)s are disruptions in the status quo that compel prospects to seek out life or career changes. For some prospects, windows of enlistment opportunity are predictable because they are driven by the Annual Recruiting Cycle. With other grads and prior service, WEOs are less predictable and can be random. These WEOs are triggered by changes in their financial situation, employment, marital or relationship status, and other life-altering events.

Most social networks allow you to follow people without being directly connected to them. The major social networks also provide updates on the people you are following. It is important to consistently monitor your news stream and discussions in the groups where your prospects hang out. When you notice a change, that's usually a good time to contact your prospect.

Research and Information Gathering

Social media is a smorgasbord of data. You can gather an impressive amount of information about prospects that you can use for initial qualifying, developing prospecting messages, and pre-interview planning. All of the major social media channels offer powerful search capabilities that give you access to detailed information about prospects.

For social research shortcuts, I highly recommend picking up a copy of Sam Richter's book, *Take the Cold Out of Cold Calling.* Sam's book is the bible on using online and social resources to gather information.

Outbound Prospecting

Social media in-boxes may be leveraged to engage prospects directly to ask for interviews or qualifying information. When sending social in-box messages, for best results, follow the Four-Step E-Mail Prospecting Framework from the previous chapter.

The Five Cs of Social Recruiting

Mastering the five Cs of social recruiting is the key to turning intention into action and results.

Connecting

For centuries, highly successful people have understood the power of connections and how to leverage these connections to accomplish their goals. Connections get you in front of the right prospects, which helps you make mission faster.

Everything on social media begins with a connection. When you meet prospects by phone and in person, you've opened the door to familiarity. At the moment after they've just met you, you have the highest probability that they will accept your social connection request. By sending them the connection request just after they've met you, they see your name again, anchoring familiarity.

On most social platforms, once a person connects with you, you gain the ability to see their connections, which helps you gain deeper insight into their core motivations, values, and peers.

There are three ways to create connections:

- **Direct:** On Facebook, you may initiate a direct request for a connection. On Facebook, the process is straightforward: You just click "Send a Friend Request." On LinkedIn (primarily used for connections with community partners, educators, prior service, and grads who may be working in the private sector), you have the option of sending a standard, generic connection request (you may be asked to say how you know the person) or you may customize your connection request. I highly recommend sending a personalized note with each connection request that references any past meetings or conversations and gives a reason for your connection request.
- **Reciprocal:** With Twitter, Instagram, and Snapchat, you can gain connections by simply following people because when you follow, people will reciprocate and follow you back. The probability that they will reciprocate is determined by their level of familiarity with you, so it makes sense to follow people as soon as you meet them.
- **Passive:** When you publish content that connects with your audience and is shared, people will connect with and follow you. This is the most powerful way to build conections; the person connecting with you is consciously choosing to add you to their network because they believe you add value to their life.

Content Creation

Creating and publishing original content that is relevant to the issues and problems your prospects are facing is the most powerful way to build trust and credibility with your prospect base. Content will typically be in the form of:

- Pictures and memes
- Videos
- Articles

Publishing relevant content draws prospects to you and entices them to engage with you or share your message with others. When people who were previously unknown to you like or share your content, it reveals new prospects.

You also gain insight into trigger events and buying windows. When people like, comment on, or share your information, you learn about the problems they are facing, their emotions, urgency, and interest in the military.

Creating high-quality original content is powerful, but it is also very, very difficult. It requires a significant investment of time and intellectual resources. You also need to ensure that anything you post that is original is in *compliance* with regulations.

I highly recommend investing the time to create and publish original content because the benefits to your reputation and career are massive. But if developing original content is not your thing, it is easier to leverage content through curation.

Content Curation

Intuitively, we know that recruiters who connect, educate, offer insight, and solve problems are far more successful than those whose primary recruiting strategy is to slap shot features and benefits.

In the social channel, the primary way you provide value for prospects is through content that educates, builds credibility, anchors familiarity, and positions you as a trustworthy expert. The right content shared at the right time with the right prospects can create important connections and convert passive online relationships into real-time conversations.

The challenge is that the social channel is a voracious and insatiable beast that devours content. It must be fed daily for you and your message to remain relevant and present. Even if you had the time to create loads of original content, it would never be enough to keep up. So the solution is *curation*.

A simple analogy for curation is the act of clipping articles from magazines and newspapers and sending them to someone. Except on social media, you are doing this digitally and amplifying the impact by going from a one-to-one analog footprint to a one-to-many digital distribution.

Instead of publishing your own original content, you leverage the content that is being created and published by others. Essentially you become a maven who aggregates the most relevant content for your audience and shares it through your various social media newsfeeds.

Sharing can either be a direct link that you post or a share from a source you follow. The beautiful thing about sharing content is that even though you didn't produce it, some of the credit for the content rubs off on you.

To become a successful curator, you need to be aware of what is happening in your branch of the military and the military in general. Have your eyes and ears open, pay attention to what is going on around you, and consume both military and general career planning information. The branches of the military produce a massive amount of positive content that may be leveraged on your social channels.

Tools including Google Alerts, Pocket, or Feedly make it easy to stay informed and gather insightful content to share.

When you curate with intent, you begin linking together relevant content based on an overall strategy, rather than just randomly and disparately sharing. You take time to read and understand what you are sharing, which allows you to add comments and insightful takeaways to the shared content, which further burnishes your expert status.

Conversion

Let's get real. You want the time and effort you invest in social recruiting to produce real, tangible results. You want more qualified applicants in your funnel. Otherwise, what's the point?

When leveraged effectively, the social channel can and should generate inbound leads. Social recruiting, leveraged effectively, is like building your own inbound marketing machine.

This is where *intent* and strategy with content creation and curation come into play. You must actively plan for and work to generate leads and engagement that open recruiting conversations.

Consistency

Social recruiting is a grind. It takes work. It is not easy, simple, or automatic. Getting value from and adding value to the social channel requires a consistent, focused, and disciplined approach. Consistency is crucial. Social recruiting doesn't work if you show up *some* of the time. You dilute your efforts if you are random and hit-or-miss.

Time blocking is the key to being efficient. You must block 30 minutes to an hour each day (preferably before or after the Golden Hours) to engage in planned, intentional social recruiting activities. Have the discipline to limit your activity to the block of time you have set aside for social media and no more.

You may feel that you are not accomplishing much in short daily social recruiting blocks, but the cumulative impact of daily activity is enormous over time.

Social Recruiting + Outbound Prospecting = A Powerful Combination

Here's the problem you face: In the ocean of content flooding the social channel, it's getting more and more difficult to stand out and get noticed (which is why the social channels are making so much money selling sponsored posts). If you are starting from the ground up with no followers or a small audience on established social platforms like Facebook, it can take from six months to two years to create enough gravity to pull prospects in to you.

This does not mean that a targeted and narrowly focused social recruiting strategy can't be effective. It just means that it will require more and more effort to get a reasonable return on your investment. This is why a combination of social and outbound prospecting strategies is so powerful.

Outbound prospecting and inbound social recruiting go together like mashed potatoes and gravy. Social recruiting builds familiarity, is awesome for research and WEO awareness, and will generate inbound leads. It is, however, a long-term, passive strategy that requires patience and nuance and is unlikely to produce immediate results or to ever scale to a size that generates enough inbound leads to allow you to consistently make mission.

Outbound prospecting, on the other hand, is an active approach to filling the pipe by engaging prospects in person, by phone, by e-mail, through social in-boxes, or by text. It is the art of interrupting your prospect's day, opening a conversation, setting an appointment, or gathering information.

Combined with social prospecting, outbound activity becomes enormously powerful. The combined benefits include:

- Amplifying familiarity, which increases the probability that your prospect will engage.
- More targeted prospecting lists focused on the highest-qualified prospects.
- Leveraging WEOs and trigger events to engage prospects at just the right time.
- Nurturing and educating prospects ahead of expected or projected WEOs.

- Qualifying.
- Refining and making your outbound prospecting message relevant.

Once again, it comes back to balance—balancing your prospecting channels, methodologies, and techniques to be efficient and effective with your scarcest resource: *time.*

Creating Obligation and Leveraging the Law of Reciprocity with Social Media

This past summer while riding a bus in Kyoto, Japan, with my son, we struck up a conversation with a young Japanese businessman. Conversation might be an exaggeration. Since we don't speak Japanese and he didn't speak English, communication was a struggle. The one thing we found in common was music. We all took turns naming our favorite bands. Thumbs up, thumbs down. We laughed and sneered, sang snippets of songs, and enjoyed the moment—a brief connection on a hot crowded bus.

As the bus approached the next stop, the young businessman prepared to get off. The bus slowed and the doors opened. As we bowed to say goodbye, he reached into this backpack and pulled out a small, wrapped box, motioning for me to take it. At first, I politely refused, but he was emphatic that I take the gift, so I smiled, bowed, and took the box from his hand as he slipped out of the open door.

Thirty minutes later my son and I made it back to the small apartment we were renting. I peeled the green wrapping paper from the box, curious to see what was inside. When I opened the lid, it wasn't what I was expecting.

Inside were five slices of raw fish wrapped in leaves. I stared into the box in disbelief and then after a moment, reached in and pulled out a leaf-wrapped piece of fish.

My son turned up his nose as I popped it into my mouth. "Daddy, you can't eat that!" he pleaded. "That's raw fish out of some random guy's backpack from a bus. You don't know what you're putting in your mouth."

"But he gave it to me as a gift," I shot back. "I can't waste it. That wouldn't be right. It was probably his dinner!" Even though my son's argument was rational, I felt a deep emotional obligation to reciprocate the stranger's gift by eating the fish.

But my compelling feeling of obligation was far from over. The moment the young man stepped off the bus I felt a twinge of guilt. He hadn't given me time to find something in my bag to give him—to repay the favor.

It bothered me all afternoon. As we walked through the Gion district in Kyoto, I found myself looking for him, my reciprocal gift at the ready. Two months later, the guilt was still there.

This is the power of obligation. Robert B. Cialdini, author of *The Psychology of Persuasion*, says, "One of the most potent of the weapons of influence around us is the rule for reciprocation. The rule says that we should try to repay, in kind, what another person has provided us."

In layman's terms, the law of reciprocity simply explains that when someone gives you something, you feel an obligation to give value back. But as Cialdini explains, the rule or law of reciprocity goes much deeper than this. Effectively it is the glue that holds society together. This feeling of obligation, the need to reciprocate, is baked deep into our psychology.

When you follow, like, comment, and share the posts of other people, it makes them feel important. In the age of social media those likes, shares, comments, and follows are like currency. They are *gifts*.

The need for significance—to feel important—is a powerful human driver. This need is so insatiable that when you make a person feel significant, you give them the greatest gift you can give another human being. This gift is one of the cornerstones of influence. By making a person feel important, you create a subconscious feeling of obligation to reciprocate.

That desire to reciprocate will cause the other person to be more likely to share your posts—which amplifies your message. It also increases the probability that prospects will seek you out at school and community events, ask you for more information, take your call, respond to direct messages, e-mail, and text, or engage directly in conversations about a career in the military.

26

The Law of Familiarity

After seeing a lot of the world, I now tend to return to the same spots.
I enjoy the familiarity.

—Louise Nurding, singer

Staff Sergeant Sanchez plays pickup basketball three days a week at a local high school. It keeps him in shape and in touch.

During these early-morning, before-school pickup games, Sanchez interacts with potential recruits on an entirely different level. He competes, jokes, and listens. He becomes familiar to the students and moves into their "in-group."

They open up to him and introduce him to their friends. In hallways at school they smile and say hello. At after-school functions and athletic competitions, they freely introduce him to their parents. During events at school and in the community, they walk up to his table and say hello.

Sanchez is a reliably consistent producer. More than half of his enlistments come directly from the relationships he makes playing basketball.

The in-group preference (also called the similarity bias) causes your prospects to believe that people who are more familiar or more like them are more trustworthy and believable than people who are not. You know this to be true as surely as you know the sun will come up in the morning, because you face and fight this bias every day of your life.

Each of us lives and operates in a familiarity bubble. We are more comfortable with people, places, and things inside our familiarity bubble and less comfortable with things outside our familiarity bubble. Your ultimate goal, through your marketing efforts, school and community outreach activities, and consistent daily prospecting is to move into your prospects' bubble of familiarity.

The lack of familiarity is why you get so many objections. When prospects don't know you, it's much harder to get them to engage.

The more familiar prospects are with you and your branch of the military, the more likely they will engage in recruiting conversations, be open to answering your qualifying questions, introduce you to their parents (and other members of their circle of influence) and ultimately enlist.

Familiarity breeds liking.

Familiarity Reduces Friction and Resistance

It's in your best interest to invest time and effort to build familiarity with prospects, their parents, educators, administrators, and community partners. Familiarity is the lubricant of recruiting conversations. It makes the decision to spend time with you feel less risky.

There even comes a point when a prospect will readily communicate and build a "first-name" relationship with you—even when they aren't interested in enlisting at the moment. This is called the *familiarity threshold*.

When you earn enough trust to cross the familiarity threshold, you also gain the ability to communicate more freely—including through social media in-boxes and text messaging—without being considered intrusive. These prospects will introduce you to their friends and give you referrals. As educators and administrators become more familiar with you, they will open up their classrooms and their schools.

Crossing the familiarity threshold requires a significant investment of time, intellect, emotion, energy, and technology. This is why you must develop a strategy and get organized so that you focus your time and attention on daily prospecting activity that builds familiarity with your most valuable prospects, schools, and community partners.

Five Levers of Familiarity

Their success with crossing the familiarity threshold with prospects is why top recruiters like Staff Sergeant Sanchez make it look so easy. The investment they've made in building familiarity in their territory has paid off. These are five levers they pull to build familiarity:

Persistent and Consistent Prospecting

The first step in creating familiarity is through persistent and consistent daily prospecting. Each time you call, e-mail, send a text message, engage face to face, hand out a business card or brochure, leave a voice mail, or connect on social media, you create familiarity.

This is one of the core reasons why persistence pays off. The more times people see or hear your name, the more familiar you become to them and the people who influence and protect them. Simply put, the more you prospect, the more familiar you get.

Referrals and Introductions

The most powerful and direct path to familiarity is a referral or introduction. The referral gives you instant credibility because you get to ride in on the coattails of a person who is already trusted by your prospect. There are three basic types of referrals:

1. **Referrals that come from recruits you have already enlisted.** The key to generating these referrals is developing a disciplined, systematic process for staying in touch with the people you have enlisted, teaching them what you are looking for, and *asking* for referrals.
2. **Referrals that come from prospects and applicants.** When you are engaging prospects and applicants—whether qualified or not—you should always be *asking* for referrals.
3. **Referrals that come from relationships you've developed with educators, administrators, and people in your community.** To generate these referrals, you must seek out and make an ongoing investment in professional relationships. The wider your professional network, the more referrals you'll generate. The RISS is a key tool for managing these relationships.

The real secret to generating referrals is:

Step 1: Invest in relationships

Step 2: Ask

That's it. Straightforward and simple. Yet, while standing in front of a group of recruiters last month, I asked:

"How many of you asked for at least one referral last week?"

No hands went up.

"How about in the last month?"

One hand.

"How about in the last quarter?"

Three hands.

Shocking? Not really. I ask this question to groups of recruiters regularly. The response is almost always the same.

Yet referrals are your easiest enlistments. They are more likely to engage, more likely to be qualified, and less likely to hit you with objections. Developing a consistent stream of referrals makes mission far more attainable.

I'm not going to waste your time discussing why recruiters don't ask, because that answer is more than obvious: They either fear getting turned down (rejection) or they have not developed the intentional habit of asking everyone they meet for referrals.

This brings us back to the most important discipline in recruiting—*asking*. The key to getting referrals is the discipline to ask, and the more times you ask, the more referrals you will get.

School Activities

The heart of military recruiting is the high school. This is where familiarity is born. This is where relationships are conceived. Success in the grad market is critically dependent on the relationships you build with students while they are still in high school. So you've got to be cool to your schools.

But you must *go!* Can I make this any clearer? Go to your schools. Go shake hands. Go meet people. Go learn about them. Go get involved. Go seek out opportunities to help.

Involvement allows you to engage students on a different level. Most schools are running on thin budgets. They need help. If you volunteer, they'll allow you to help coach sports, or be a substitute teacher, or help with graduation and other activities. Many recruiters become such an integral part of their schools that students and teachers think they work there. It's a powerful position to be in as a recruiter.

Events and Networking

Nothing breeds familiarity better than face-to-face contact. Social media prospecting is important, but events and face-to-face networking are the real social recruiting.

Whether it's playing pickup basketball, volunteering in your schools and communities, going to sporting events, attending local community events—there are endless opportunities to network in your community and school.

Events help you create connections with prospects and make it much easier to qualify them with greater transparency. You create connections when you ask questions, listen, and become genuinely interested in other people. Maya Angelou said, "People will forget what you said or did, but they will always remember how you made them feel." Take this to heart as you invest time in networking and events and refrain from being a walking, talking marketing brochure.

Following up after events is the key to anchoring new relationships and familiarity. Use handwritten notes to remind the other person of your conversation by referencing something you spoke about. Keep a stack of stamped envelopes and thank-you notes in your car. Write notes while the conversations are still fresh.

After a positive conversation, send a short text to thank the person for taking time to speak with you. Follow that up with a social media connection request to further anchor familiarity.

Finally, log any leads into your Recruiting Information Support System no later than the next morning. If you promised to send something, schedule an appointment, or introduce them to someone else, schedule a task and take action within 24 hours of the event.

Then follow up on a regular basis until you move these prospects into the pipeline.

Personal Branding and Marketing

Familiarity is also built through personal branding—making a direct investment in improving the awareness of your name, face, and reputation. This is the ultimate way to build familiarity because people enlist with *you* first, then the military.

The military marketing machine is always at work, driving brand recognition and generating leads through traditional advertising, social media, and content marketing. But you have a role to play as well. You must actively participate in getting the word out about *you* and career opportunities within your branch.

Never in the human experience has it been easier to build familiarity through personal branding. Today, distributing content is easy. Just jump on your favorite social network and go to town. Point, shoot, write, click, and publish—it's all at your fingertips. You can get your name out there and build your reputation fast.

There is, however, a personal branding methodology that is so little used that I consider it a secret weapon in the war for familiarity. It has an extraordinary track record for producing results and creates instant familiarity, credibility, and leads.

The secret: Speak in public, regularly.

Public speaking is a powerful method for meeting people and developing relationships because it creates a situation where prospects seek you out.

When you speak in public, at least for a moment, you are considered a minor celebrity who people want to meet. After you give your speech, people walk up to you, engage you in conversations, open up freely, and voluntarily hand over their contact information.

You can easily get speaking gigs. Organizations like the chamber of commerce, Rotary Club, trade organizations, schools, colleges, and other civic groups are always in need of guest speakers. All you really have to do is call and volunteer and they will happily put you on the schedule.

Speaking allows you to tell your personal story and showcase your knowledge and experience in the military. It gives you tremendous visibility and credibility. It sets you apart, enhances your personal brand, and creates a greater sense of familiarity with your prospects.

Remember, though, like everything in recruiting, building familiarity is about balance. You must balance the need for enlistments today with an investment in the future.

PART IX | Charlie Mike

27 | Mission Drive

I offer neither pay, nor quarters, nor food; I offer only hunger, thirst, forced marches, battles, and death. Let him who loves his country with his heart, and not merely with his lips, follow me.
  —Giuseppe Garibaldi, Italian military leader

The remnants of what was once an army stood shivering in the sleet and freezing rain on a frigid Christmas day. Casualties from a string of defeats had shrunk the ranks by more than two-thirds.

To say that nothing was going well would be an understatement. The army had been outflanked by the forces of its enemy at every turn, supplies were razor thin, and it was teetering on the edge of total collapse.

The remaining soldiers were worn out. Many had no shoes and little in the way of coats and blankets to protect them from the brutal winter weather. On paper the situation was dire, with little hope.

The commanding General needed more men. He had dispatched recruiters to find fresh replacements and agonized over how to retain the soldiers whose enlistments would be up in another five days. He begged his government for the resources he needed to retain them.

The political leaders, though, were blind to just how close their army and country were to total defeat. Instead of sending resources, they bickered and argued over mundane issues. And following his defeats, loss of territory, and nearly constant retreat, the politicians were beginning to doubt the General.

Though he revealed this to no one, the General was beginning to doubt himself as well. Was he the right man for the moment? Could he keep his disintegrating army intact? Could he pull back from the brink and save his nation?

He'd sacrificed everything for this mission. Failure would mean losing his land, wealth, family, life, and honor. It would extinguish the dream of freedom that both he and his men shared. And though the way forward was more uncertain than ever, there was no going back. The "ships had been burned." For the General, and his remaining patriots, failure was unthinkable.

As the men stepped into the wooden boats at the edge of the ice-filled river for a bold assault on their enemy on the other shore, their drive to complete the mission was unassailable.

The Four Pillars of Mission Drive

Military recruiting can be described as long stretches of adversity, pain, heartache, and suck interrupted by brief moments of elation. In this grueling environment, it's challenging to wake up each day driven to hit the phones, streets, and schools on the hunt for your next Alpha.

It is difficult to find the motivation to go the extra mile for an applicant, chase down transcripts, deal with yet another MEPS waiver, calm another hysterical mom, and wade through the excruciating bureaucracy.

Many military recruiters crack in this environment. They grow cynical and negative. Make excuses for poor performance. Hide from the truth, underperform, and in the process hurt their fellow service members, family, and country.

In their frustration, they see only an arbitrary number (mission) handed down from above. They don't see or connect to any purpose in their role. Therefore, in the midst of adversity and pain, they have difficulty finding the motivation to embrace the suck that is military recruiting and attack each day as a fierce, driven warrior to win the War for Talent.

General Douglas MacArthur said, "It's fatal to enter a war without the will to win it." If you don't know *why* you do this job, it's impossible to remain motivated in the face of adversity. This is the reason why ultra-high performance in military recruiting begins and ends with *Mission Drive*.

- Mission drive is the common discipline shared by all ultra-high performers.
- Mission drive is more important than talent, experience, education, skills, or technique.
- Mission drive is why some recruiters thrive under pressure while others with the same level of talent fold up like a cheap lawn chair as soon as things get difficult.

Despite the highly stressful, high-pressure environment, ultra-high performers have a relaxed confidence. They fully expect to succeed. They believe they control their future. They display optimism in the face of adversity. They adapt, innovate, and persevere. They have an undying will and determination to win the War for Talent. Ultra-high performers gain their competitive edge from this unquenchable drive.

Mission drive is built and developed on four foundational pillars:

1. Optimism
2. Competitiveness
3. Need for Achievement
4. Purpose

Optimism

Fanatical military recruiters have a winning, optimistic mind-set. They know that negative, bitter people with a victim mind-set do not succeed in recruiting. They attack each day with enthusiasm—fired up and ready to rock.

They seize the day, brush past naysayers and complainers, and dive into recruiting with unequaled drive. Even on bad days, they reach deep inside and find enough stored enthusiasm to push themselves to keep going to make one more call.

The positive feeling of optimism helps you face adversity and keep going. When you get knocked down, optimism tells you that if you can look up, you can get up. Optimism helps you forget rejection fast. It is the mother of perseverance. It powers a positive belief system and attracts positive energy.

As General Colin Powell so aptly stated, "Perpetual optimism is a force multiplier."

Competitiveness

Do you hate to lose or love to win? The drive to avoid losing is what keeps ultra-high performers working longer and harder and doing what it takes to win. Competitiveness is the mother of persistence. It is a critical component on the daily battlefield of the War for Talent.

Fanatical military recruiters view recruiting through the eyes of a fierce competitor. They are hardwired to win and will do whatever it takes to stay on top. They begin each day prepared to win the battle for the attention of the most coveted prospects and to outwit and outhustle their competitors at every turn.

Fanatical military recruiters approach prospects, parents, educators, and community partners with confidence. They expect to win and believe in mission. They have developed mental toughness and the ability to manage the disruptive emotions of fear, insecurity, uncertainty, and doubt. They leverage confidence and self-control to persuade prospects to give up time to engage in conversations and interviews.

Need for Achievement

Fanatical military recruiters have a high need for achievement. Psychologist and researcher Henry Murray defined the need for achievement as "intense, prolonged and repeated efforts to accomplish something difficult. To work with singleness of purpose toward a high and distant goal. To have the determination to win."[1]

The need for achievement is the mother of self-motivation.[2] Recruiters with a high need for achievement are biased toward action. They are driven to win. They never, ever give up believing, at the core, that persistence always prevails. They use rejection as fuel to get up and keep moving with a determined belief that their next "yes" is right around the corner.

Purpose

An uncomfortable unspoken truth is that no one can *order* you to recruit. No one can *order* you to make mission.

How do I know? Simple. If ordering worked in recruiting, I wouldn't be writing this book, because 100 percent of recruiters would be delivering 100 percent of mission 100 percent of the time.

Now, don't get me wrong. Your NCOIC can order you to sit at your desk, call a list, or go to a school. You can be ordered to follow process and procedures.

But no one can order you to be confident in the face of rejection, to be a fanatical prospector, to demonstrate empathy and poise. Under *orders* you'll go through the motions, but without *drive* you won't be successful or happy.

The writer G.K. Chesterton once said that "The true soldier fights not because he hates what is in front of him, but because he loves what is behind him."

I want you to stop for a moment and look at yourself in the mirror. See yourself for who you really are. You have the most important, mission-critical role in the military and (I argue) the country.

The truth is that for our voluntary military, no recruiters = no military = no America. It is that simple and that brutal. Our democracy and unique way of life depend on *you*. Your children and grandchildren depend on you. Everything rests on your success in engaging and enlisting the most talented men and women to serve and protect our country.

Napoleon Hill, who wrote self-help books, once said that desire [purpose] is the starting point of all achievement: not a hope, not a wish, but a keen pulsating desire that transcends everything. For military recruiters, *purpose* is at the heart of *Mission Drive.*

To be an effective recruiter, you must understand, nurture, and harness your purpose or *why*. You must discover and internalize the reason *why* you do this job. And to truly harness purpose for motivational drive, your *why* must transcend orders or a paycheck or a required step for promotion. It must be bigger than these transactional things.

Purpose is the singularity of achievement. Anything truly worth achieving must begin with purpose. Otherwise you'll fail. It's the key to tapping into the motivation you need to get past real and self-inflicted performance roadblocks. It's easier to develop the mental toughness, resilience, and self-discipline required to be an ultra-high-performing military recruiter when you have a strong sense of purpose.

In the space below, take a moment now to define and write down your *why*—what drives you as a military recruiter:

Embrace the Suck—You Have to Grind to Shine

Prospecting creates adversity. There will be hurdles, roadblocks, disappointment, and loads of rejection. There will always be a mountain you'll have to climb and an uphill battle you'll have to fight. There will always be a temptation to slack off. There will always be an excuse for why you can't do something.

In military recruiting, there are only three things you can control:

1. **Actions**—what you choose to do each day and every moment.
2. **Reactions**—how you respond to people, circumstances, and disruptive emotions.
3. **Mind-set**—your attitude and beliefs.

Losing is a choice. Thousands upon thousands of recruiters fail and are miserable because they make the choice—yes, the choice—to lose.

Mediocrity is a choice. When you choose mediocre behaviors, you get mediocre results, and once you allow mediocrity into your recruiting day, you become a bad-luck magnet.

A poor attitude or a poor belief system is a choice. This choice is one of the key reasons so many recruiters find themselves stressed out, negative, and miserable.

Despite the extensive training given to them in recruiting school, despite the coaching and mentoring given by peers and leaders, despite the tools and technology, these recruiters wallow in mediocrity and failure.

Quitting is a choice. Most people, when faced with challenges, quit too soon—often right as they are on the cusp of success. This is especially true with new recruiters.

Starting your tour as a military recruiter is frustratingly hard. There are many dark days when you feel like all you do is fail and there is no hope. As you get closer to breaking through, things can seem bleaker. You are tired, beat-up, and worn down. It is at this point that mental toughness, resilience, persistence, and faith take you the last mile.

British Prime Minister Winston Churchill said that "when you are going through hell, keep going." Faith is crucial. Faith that by doing the right things every day, the cumulative impact of these actions will pay off. Faith keeps you focused on mission when no tangible evidence exists that the hard work you are doing will pay off.

Persistence is the fuel of winners. It is the tenacity and determination to keep going in spite of self-doubt, roadblocks, failure, embarrassment, and setbacks. Persistence picks you up off the ground, dusts you off, and sends you back into the game. Persistence gives you that last push across the finish line.

The fact is, military recruiting is a never-ending grind. But you've got to grind to shine.

Everybody wants glory, but most people are unwilling to grind—to pay the price for success. In any endeavor, success is paid for in advance with hard work. In recruiting, success is paid for in advance with prospecting. You will never excel at anything if you don't put the hard work in first.

The top people in business, sports, recruiting, and every other walk of life hit the same walls and face the same mental and physical suffering as everyone else. What makes them different is their ability to lean into their challenges and disrupt the desire to quit—to sacrifice what they want *now* for what they want *most*.

Mission drive cuts through any delusion that things will be easy, embraces the "suck"—and in recruiting, what sucks is prospecting.

The Enduring Mantra of Ultra-High-Performing Recruiters

Success leaves clues. If you study what successful people do, you find patterns. When you duplicate those patterns, you'll be able to duplicate their success. The path to consistently delivering on mission is simple and straightforward. Simple, mind you—not easy.

Over the course of this book, I've taken you on an unprecedented journey into many of the behaviors and mind-sets of elite military recruiters. You've learned a set of techniques, frameworks, and processes that lead to ultra-high performance.

Like most military recruiters, ultra-high performers possess a solid understanding of recruiting techniques and skills. Likewise, they have knowledge, systems, and understanding of the recruiting process. What sets them apart is their unrelenting command and mastery of five core disciplines:

1. **Prospecting discipline:** Ultra-high performance begins with relentless and unstoppable prospecting. UHPs leverage a balanced methodology to consistently keep the recruiting pipeline full of qualified applicants. Quite simply, they talk to and engage more people than anyone else.

2. **Time discipline:** UHPs are efficient and effective, accomplishing more, in less time, with greater outcomes. They understand that time is the most valuable currency in recruiting—time is mission—and that how they choose to use their time is the greatest limiter of success.

3. **Probability discipline:** Because time is limited and precious, UHPs invest their time with qualified prospects who have the highest probability of enlisting and shipping. Win probability is how UHPs play the game of recruiting. Every action UHPs take, every move on the board, is calculated to bend the win probability in their favor.

4. **Emotional discipline:** In each recruiting conversation, the person who exerts the greatest emotional control has the highest probability of getting their desired outcome. To be effective, you must learn to manage your own disruptive emotions while influencing the behaviors of others. This requires self-awareness, self-control, and empathy.

   In this age of distraction and fleeting attention spans, UHPs deploy a new psychology of recruiting (Military Recruiting EQ) to engage and influence the behaviors of prospects, applicants, parents, educators, and community partners. They master their own emotions while responding appropriately to the emotions of others in the context of the unique military recruiting conversation.

5. **Mission Drive:** UHPs possess a strong sense of purpose. They are motivated, driven, determined to perform at the highest level, and have the resilience to move past roadblocks, pain, excuses, and adversity to achieve mission. The thin line separating elite military recruiters from everyone else is *Mission Drive.*

The Mantra of Fanatical Military Recruiting

I don't remember where I found the eleven words that changed my career. What I do remember is the words resonated with me instantly:

When it is time to go home, make one more call.

I wrote the sentence on an index card and taped it over my desk. It was always the last thing I looked at before I hit the streets each day.

Those words became my mantra. On days when I was dragging my ass because I'd had it handed to me by rude prospects; when it was hot, cold, raining, or snowing; when I was tired, worn out, and burned out; or when I was coming up with really "good" justifications to knock off early for the day, this mantra, "When it is time to go home, make one more call," kept me going for one more call (and sometimes two, three, or four).

The impact of those extra calls was mind blowing. So many of my "one more calls" turned into winners. It was as if the universe was rewarding me for sticking to it. The more I prospected, the luckier I became. I had success I would have never realized if I had not developed the discipline to make one more call.

Fanatical military recruiters have the self-discipline to do the hard things in recruiting. They understand that to succeed at the highest level, they must pay for mission in advance with hard work, sacrifice, pain, and doing things they hate.

And, when it's time to go home. . . . When they are tired and hungry. . . . When there is nothing left to give. . . . When they've had all the rejection they can take, they push themselves to keep going and make **one more call**.

Charlie Mike

At 3:00 a.m. on December 26, 1776, General George Washington gathered up his rag-tag troops on the New Jersey side of the Delaware River and began the march on Trenton. They had crossed the river in heavy flat-bottomed boats in a full-on northeaster—men, cannon, and horses—in gale-force winds.

It had taken hours to get everyone across (longer than antici-pated, putting them behind plan). The men were freezing cold, lay-ered in ice, and bordering on hypothermia. The Continental Army looked more like a mob of paupers than an army.

Washington knew he was taking a huge gamble. The storm had set them back. They were three hours behind schedule and had, most likely, lost the element of surprise. Downstream, his diver-sionary and flanking forces, battered by the storm, had been unable to cross the river.

He was on his own.

For Washington, adversity always seemed to fuel his drive. Before leaving for battle he wrote, "It is vain to ruminate upon, or even reflect upon the authors of our present misfortune. We should rather exert ourselves, and look forward with hopes, that some lucky chance may yet turn up in our favor." And when he fell behind schedule in that frigid northeaster, when his other commanding officers had given up and taken shelter, he explained to John Hancock that "I was determined to push on at all events."[3]

The dream of freedom and escape from tyranny was at stake. Defeat on this day might mean the end of the American democracy before it ever really began. He was pushing himself and his soldiers beyond what was humanly possible for this cause and purpose. It drove him—a perpetual hunger.

The march to Trenton was slow and grueling. The men, silent in the darkness, moved forward at a child's pace, on slick frozen ground, suffering from the bitter cold and lack of sleep, the wind howling. Washington's *lucky chance* was that the commander of the Hessian forces, Colonel Johann Rall, did not anticipate that the Americans would attack in this kind of weather.

At 8:00 a.m. the Continental Army attacked Trenton. Even though the men were weary and frozen to the bone, they, in Washington's words, "seemed to vie with the other in pressing forward."

The attack was a total surprise for the elite Hessian mercenaries, holed up in their winter quarters, still fat on Christmas cheer. The battle was savage, swift, and decisive—over in just 45 minutes.

In the aftermath, 21 Hessians lay dead, 90 wounded, and almost a thousand were captured along with sorely needed supplies. Only four Americans had been wounded.

On that day, Washington and his men who, in the words of John Handcock, were "broken by fatigue and ill-fortune" changed the course of history. They gave hope to a country that had been demoralized by defeat.

As news of the victory spread far and wide, a wave of new recruits bolstered the ranks. Yet, there was still the problem of how to retain the troops whose enlistments were expiring on December 31. Holding on to his veterans and keeping his army together were Washington's most pressing concerns following the improbable victory at Trenton.

On December 30, he addressed his men:

> My brave fellows, you have done all I asked you to do, and more than could be reasonably expected, but your country is at stake, your wives, houses, and all that you hold dear. You have worn yourselves out with fatigues and hardships, but we know not how to spare you. If you will consent to stay one month longer, you will render that service to the cause of liberty, and to your country, which you can probably never do under any other circumstance.

Gandhi once said that a small body of determined spirits fired by an unquenchable faith in their mission can alter the course of history. When Washington finished speaking and the drums sounded, the men stepped forward. And though history books don't always record it so, that was the moment when America was truly born.

Notes

I Go to Basic

1. https://www.armytimes.com/news/your-army/2017/10/12/
   top-recruiter-just-136000-out-of-33-million-young-americans-
   would-join-the-army/.

Chapter 1: Military Recruiting Is Facing a Perfect Storm

1. http://www.pewresearch.org/fact-tank/2012/02/02/large-
   military-civilian-gap-among-young-americans/.
2. http://www.latimes.com/nation/la-na-warrior-main-
   20150524-story.html.
3. http://www.pewresearch.org/fact-tank/2017/04/13/6-facts-
   about-the-u-s-military-and-its-changing-demographics/.
4. https://www.cfr.org/article/demographics-us-military.
5. http://www.latimes.com/nation/la-na-warrior-main-
   20150524-story.html.
6. http://www.pewsocialtrends.org/2011/11/23/the-military-
   civilian-gap-fewer-family-connections/.
7. Pew Research Center 2012.
8. http://www.pewresearch.org/fact-tank/2016/10/18/most-
   americans-trust-the-military-and-scientists-to-act-in-the-
   publics-interest/.

Chapter 5: Effective Recruiting Begins with the Discipline to Ask

1. From the movie *The Big Short*.

Chapter 6: How to Ask

1. Wang, Shirley, "Contagious Behavior," *Observer* 19:2 (2006). Available at Association for Psychological Science, https://www .psychologicalscience.org/observer/contagious-behavior.

Chapter 8: The Three Ps That Are Holding You Back

1. Carolyn Gregoire, "Fourteen Signs Your Perfectionism Has Gotten Out of Control," *Huffington Post*, www.huffingtonpost .com/2013/11/06/why-perfectionism-is-ruin_n_4212069.html.

Chapter 9: Time Discipline

1. "'I Lost It': The Boss Who Banned Phones, and What Came Next." https://www.wsj.com/articles/can-you-handle-it-bosses-ban-cellphones-from-meetings-1526470250.

Chapter 11: *Yes* Has a Number

1. https://www.mathsisfun.com/numbers/ratio.html.

Chapter 19: The Science Behind the Hurt

1. A 2011 brain-imaging study published in the *Proceedings of the National Academy of Sciences* shows that social rejection and physical pain both prompt activity in the brain regions of the secondary somatosensory cortex and the dorsal posterior insula.

And a study published in 2017 in the journal *Social Cognitive and Affective Neuroscience* shows that the posterior insular cortex and secondary somatosensory cortex parts of the brain are activated both when we experience social rejection and when we witness others experiencing social rejection.

2. A small study from University of Michigan medical school researchers also showed that the brain's mu-opioid receptor system releases natural painkillers, or opioids, in response to social pain. This happens to be the same system that releases opioids in the face of physical pain. See "Social rejection shares somatosensory representations with physical pain" by Ethan Krossa, Marc G. Berman, Walter Mischel, Edward E. Smith, and Tor D. Wager, http://www .pnas.org/content/108/15/6270.full.pdf.

3. Guy Winch, *Emotional First Aid: Healing Rejection, Guilt, Failure, and Other Everyday Hurts* (New York: Plume, 2014).

4. http://ideas.ted.com/why-rejection-hurts-so-much-and-what-to-do-about-it/.

5. https://www.psychologytoday.com/blog/the-squeaky-wheel/201307/10-surprising-facts-about-rejection.

6. https://www.psychologytoday.com/blog/the-squeaky-wheel/201307/10-surprising-facts-about-rejection.

Chapter 20: Rejection Proof

1. Jia Jiang, *Rejection Proof* (New York: Harmony Books, 2015).

2. Scott G. Halford, *Activate Your Brain: How Understanding Your Brain Can Improve Your Work—and Your Life* (Austin, TX: Greenleaf Book Group Press, 2015).

3. http://www.nytimes.com/2014/02/23/sports/olympics/olympians-use-imagery-as-mental-training.html?_r=0.

4. http://www.sportpsychologytoday.com/sport-psychology-for-coaches/the-power-of-visualization/.

5. http://www.huffingtonpost.com/2014/03/13/rejection-coping-methods-research_n_4919538.html.

6. http://jamesclear.com/body-language-how-to-be-confident.

7. http://lifehacker.com/the-science-behind-posture-and-how-it-affects-your-brai-1463291618.

8. https://youtu.be/Ks-_Mh1QhMc.
9. Dictionary.com.
10. https://www.outwardbound.org/.
11. https://www.spartan.com/en/race/obstacles/obstacle-details.
12. Individual differences in neural response to rejection: the joint effect of self-esteem and attentional control.

Chapter 21: Prospecting Objections

1. https://www.theguardian.com/world/2011/sep/05/september-11-road-deaths.
2. Source: National Safety Council estimates based on data from National Center for Health Statistics–Mortality Data, as compiled from data provided by the 57 vital statistics jurisdictions through the Vital Statistics Cooperative Program. Deaths are classified on the basis of the World Health Organization's The International Classification of Diseases (ICD). For additional mortality figures, and estimated one-year and lifetime odds, see Injury Facts® 2017 Edition, pages 40-43. https://www.nsc.org/work-safety/tools-resources/injury-facts/chart.
3. https://blog.nationalgeographic.org/2011/11/22/nat-geo-wild-what-are-the-odds-some-surprising-shark-attack-stats/.
4. https://msu.edu/~ema/803/Ch11-JDM/2/Tversky Kahneman73.pdf.
5. Source: National Safety Council estimates based on data from National Center for Health Statistics–Mortality Data, as compiled from data provided by the 57 vital statistics jurisdictions through the Vital Statistics Cooperative Program. Deaths are classified on the basis of the World Health Organization's The International Classification of Diseases (ICD). For additional mortality figures, and estimated one-year and lifetime odds, see Injury Facts® 2017 Edition, pages 40-43. https://www.nsc.org/work-safety/tools-resources/injury-facts/chart.
6. https://www.fool.com/investing/general/2014/03/15/dying-for-a-paycheck-these-jobs-are-more-dangerous.aspx.
7. Antonio Damasio, *Descartes' Error: Emotion, Reason, and the Human Brain* (1994; repr., Penguin Books, 2005).

8. Tara Bennett-Goleman, *Emotional Alchemy* (New York: Harmony Books, 2002).
9. Daniel Goleman, *Focus* (New York: Harper Paperbacks, 2015), p. 194.
10. http://www.instructionaldesign.org/theories/cognitive-load.html.
11. Dr. Mark P. Mattson, "Superior Pattern Processing Is the Essence of the Evolved Human Brain," *Frontiers in Neuroscience* 8 (2014): 265. http://www.ncbi.nlm.nih.gov/pmc/articles/PMC4141622/.

Chapter 22: Face-to-Face Prospecting

1. Daniel Kahneman, *Thinking, Fast and Slow* (New York: Farrar, Straus and Giroux, 2011).

Chapter 23: Text Messaging

1. Lead360, www.marketingprofs.com/charts/2013/10210/texting-prospects-at-the-right-time-boosts-conversion.

Chapter 25: Social Recruiting

1. "New Research Study Breaks Down 'The Perfect Profile Photo,'" https://www.photofeeler.com/blog/perfect-photo.php.

Chapter 27: Mission Drive

1. H. A. Murray, *Explorations in Personality* (New York: Oxford University Press, 1938).
2. Chris Croner, PhD, and Richard Abraham, *Never Hire a Bad Salesperson Again* (The Richard Abraham Company, LLC; 1st edition, 2006).
3. David McCullough, *1776* (New York: Simon & Schuster, 2005), pp. 274–76.

About the Author

Jeb Blount is the author of ten books and among the world's most respected thought leaders on human-to-human interactions in sales, leadership, and customer experience. He transforms organizations by helping people reach peak performance fast.

Through his training organization, Sales Gravy, Jeb and his team train and advise many of the world's leading organizations and their executives.

Jeb spends more than 250 days a year traveling across the globe to deliver keynote speeches, workshops, and training programs to high-performing teams and their leaders across the globe.

To schedule Jeb to speak at your next event or learn more about our military recruiting training programs:

- Call 1–888–360–2249
- E-mail james.beaty@salesgravy.com or carrie@salesgravy.com
- Visit www.jebblount.com
- Visit www.salesgravy.com
- Visit www.FanaticalRecruiting.com

You may contact Jeb directly at jeb@salesgravy.com and connect with him on LinkedIn, Twitter, Facebook, YouTube, and Instagram.

Acknowledgments

When I began this mission to write this book, I made one call. It started with, "Shannon I have this crazy idea to write a book for military recruiters."

Shannon Vargo is my Executive Editor at John Wiley & Sons. She is amazing and gives me a lot of leeway, but I knew that this book pitch would be a stretch. Military recruiting is not a large enough market to interest a big publisher like Wiley, so I expected pushback.

But Shannon didn't hesitate because she understood the mission and why this book matters so much. This is exactly why I am so deeply grateful to Shannon and the entire team at Wiley, including Matt Holt, Peter Knox, and Deborah Schindlar. Thank you for your support, trust, and patience.

Likewise, I'm in deeply in debt to Command Sergeant Rick Haerter, Captain Liz Albertson, and Sergeant First Class James Beaty (Ret) for your help with fleshing out the manuscript, editing, and ensuring that I got the language right. Thank you very, very much!

Thank you to the dozens of military recruiters, NCOICs, and commanders who contributed to building my knowledge base on military recruiting and encouraging me to write this book. There is no possible way I could have written it without you.

To my team at Sales Gravy, thank you for your passion for impacting and changing lives. I'm blessed to have you in my corner!

To Carrie, my best friend, confidant, business partner, devoted mother, and beautiful wife, thank you for going to the prom with me. I love you!

Above all, I am grateful to the men and women of the United States Armed Forces for your dedication, service, sacrifice, and for putting your lives on the line to protect and defend our way of life and precious freedom. We owe you a debt that can never be fully repaid.

Index